What People Are Saying About Unlocking Epiphany

An extremely creative book incorporating ancient philosophy, poetry, and other wisdom works. This historical view is then mixed with modern challenges that life coaches and spiritual advisors can blend with the uniqueness of every client and the skills and accepted competencies of coaching. This is indeed a book with depth, uniqueness, and stimulating knowledge for modern practitioners.
Patrick Williams, PhD, MCC, author of *Becoming a Professional Life Coach: The Art and Science of a Whole Person Approach*

What's below the surface? As coaches, we are trained to identify and listen for what is at the core of the issue. As individuals, we often don't go deep enough to find out. I love how Elizabeth-Anne has not just started the conversation around these *Epiphany Moments* but has also defined and persisted there so that we can feel comfortable navigating in this space. A truly phenomenal and insightful read.
Peter A. James, PhD, MBA, PCC, President & CEO, HCG Consulting Solutions, Inc., and author of *Everyday Is a Monday*

This helpful guide for life coaches obviously springs from a wealth of experience and knowledge. The author emphasizes the difference between coaching and therapy, gives many examples of the types of situations and clients a coach may encounter, and provides both insightful archetypes and helpful questions for navigating these situations.
Amy Florian, thanatologist, speaker, coach, and author of *A Friend Indeed: Help Those You Love When They Grieve*

In a practical, straightforward, and very readable way, Elizabeth-Anne Stewart has captured the spirit of *Unlocking Epiphany Moments in Coaching*. For new as well as experienced coaches and those in the helping professions, her insights, talent, and storytelling ability illuminate effective processes and results of what *Epiphany Moments* are and how to embody them for growth and for living more consciously, meaningfully, and purposefully.
Peter Metzner MA, MPA, PCC, BCC, President & Founder, Dynamic Change Inc.

A groundbreaking book on the power of *Epiphanies* to elevate coaching and create truly transformational results. The author draws on extensive scholarship and practical examples from her years of experience to illustrate how transcendent insights can and should be brought into result-oriented coaching.
Bill Epperly, PhD, spiritual guide, founder of Integral Awakenings, and author of *A Monk in the World* (Substack)

How can coaches help clients use an *Epiphany's* flash of insight as a doorway to deeper self-awareness? Stewart's lively and engaging primer offers practical approaches that can turn these precious moments of potential into lasting transformative change. Revealing the *Epiphany's* elusive power, this guide is an essential addition to every coach's bookshelf.
Kay Leigh Hagan, PCC, Leadership Development Coach

Well done, Elizabeth-Anne Stewart! *Unlocking Epiphany Moments* is the stepping stone to tapping into the consciousness of a Holistic Modality with a level of understanding and appreciation for Divine Archetypes and spiritual curiosity; it is this approach that will facilitate a relationship with coaches, professionals,

clients, and individuals who want to make a difference and get past the rumblings of everyday life.
Patrick Ramcharitar, CPC, ELI, CTDS, CWDS, President, Upfront Essential Coaching

I graduated from *ThrivingTogether*, an ICF-certified coach training program at Catholic Theological Union in Chicago. This course has been helpful in many ways in my work as a parish priest. People come to see me, seeking a human connection to help them see clearly the situations they find themselves in. They could search the internet for AI-based solutions to their dilemmas if all they desired were a computer printout to lead them from Point A to Point B. It has been my experience that in seeking out a coach or a pastoral person, the client is desirous of a human connection to accompany them in their exploration of their life's challenges. Computers can give efficient answers, but they are incapable of entering into heart-speaking-to-heart communication.

Dr Stewart clearly illustrates the distinction between the AI BOT and the fully engaged human coach. Her book is filled with gems of practical knowledge available to both humans and AI. The richness found in Chapter 15 points to what can only be found in the human coaching experience: the role of the "spirit," which provides inspiration to the overall dynamic between coach and client.
Rev. Brian G. Bricker, O.P., Associate Pastor, St. Pius V Church Chicago, IL

This book is a must-read for coaches hungry to expand spiritual horizons with their clients. Bearing witness to the other's *Epiphany* creates the numinous moment where the magic takes place, and sacred mysteries unfold with meaning.
DeeAnna Merz Nagel, D.Th., coeditor of *Case Studies in Spiritual Coaching: A Survey Across Life, Wellness, and Work Domains*

Unlocking Epiphany Moments

A Primer for Life Coaches and
Other Inner Guides

Unlocking Epiphany Moments

A Primer for Life Coaches and Other Inner Guides

Elizabeth-Anne Stewart

CHANGEMAKERS
BOOKS

London, UK
Washington, DC, USA

CollectiveInk

First published by Changemakers Books, 2025
Changemakers Books is an imprint of Collective Ink Ltd.,
Unit 11, Shepperton House, 89 Shepperton Road, London, N1 3DF
office@collectiveinkbooks.com
www.collectiveinkbooks.com
www.changemakers-books.com

For distributor details and how to order please visit the 'Ordering' section on our website.

Text copyright: Elizabeth-Anne Stewart 2024

ISBN: 978 1 80341 722 6
978 1 80341 882 7 (ebook)
Library of Congress Control Number: 2024939569

All rights reserved. Except for brief quotations in critical articles or reviews, no part of this book may be reproduced in any manner without prior written permission from the publishers.

The rights of Elizabeth-Anne Stewart as author have been asserted in accordance with the Copyright, Designs and Patents Act 1988.

A CIP catalogue record for this book is available from the British Library.

Design: Lapiz Digital Services

UK: Printed and bound by CPI Group (UK) Ltd, Croydon, CR0 4YY
Printed in North America by CPI GPS partners

We operate a distinctive and ethical publishing philosophy in all areas of our business, from our global network of authors to production and worldwide distribution.

Previous Books by

Elizabeth-Anne Stewart

Mind-Shifting Imagery: Image Guidance for Life Coaches
Amazon, 2018
ISBN: 9781721576302

Preaching & Teaching Laudato Si
Amazon, 2015
ISBN: 97815153788396

A Pocketful of Sundays
Chicago: Lulu Press, 2009
ISBN: 5-80003-0-792242

The Day the Fireworks Died
Malta, Europe: PEG Publishers, 2005, translated into
Maltese, *Id-Dragun Tad Dragonara*. Preca Publications, 2017
ISBN: 99909-0-420-0

Dragut's Galley
Malta, Europe: PEG Publishers, 2004
ISBN: 99909-379-4

Jesus the Holy Fool
Wisconsin: Sheed & Ward, 1999
ISBN: 1-58051-061-2

From Center to Circumference: God's Place in the Circle of Self
New Jersey: Paulist Press, 1996
ISBN: 0-8091-3623-6

Image Guidance and Healing
New Jersey: Paulist Press, 1994
ISBN: 0-8091-3508-6

Pilgrims at Heart
St. Louis, Mo: Creative Communications, 1993
ISBN: 0-9629585-3-0

Image Guidance: A Tool for Spiritual Direction
New Jersey: Paulist Press, 1992
ISBN: 978-0809133215

Woman Dreamer
Bristol, Indiana: Bristol Banner Books, 1989
ISBN: 1-55605-126-3

Extraordinary Time
Canton, Ohio: Life Enrichment Publishers, 1988.
ISBN: 0-938736-24-8

Frost and Fire
Canton, Ohio: Life Enrichment Publishers, 1985.
ISBN: 0-9378736-16-7

***

For Evelyn,
Weaver of Tapestries,
Collage Maker, Poet, Woman Observing,
Ekphrastic Writer, Colorful Gypsy,
Contemplative, Soul-Friend,
Facilitator of Epiphanies,
Perceiver of the Infinite.

***

Just because…

Contents

Introduction	1
Chapter 1: So You're Having an Epiphany Moment	5
Poem: "Reality"	21
Chapter 2: Archimedes Takes a Bath!	22
Poem: "Primeval"	30
Chapter 3: Blocks to Epiphany Moments	31
Poem: "Fragile"	38
Chapter 4: Truth Is a Kaleidoscope	39
Poem: "Witch Hunt"	47
Chapter 5: Deciphering the Subtext	48
Poem: "Roots"	54
Chapter 6: Crossing Over into the Client's Experience	56
Poem: "Cosmic Wheel"	65
Chapter 7: Unknowing and Exploring the Unknown	67
Poem: "Ambiguity"	75
Chapter 8: Rigid Mindsets	77
Poem: "Excerpt from 'Nazareth Sequences'"	84
Chapter 9: Distorted Thinking	87
Poem: "On the Stupidity of Gulls"	96

Chapter 10: Primary Addictions	97
Poem: "Dry Wood"	123
Chapter 11: That Terrifying Shadow	124
Poem: "Between Years"	133
Chapter 12: Coaching *The Shadow*	135
Poem: "Misbegotten"	154
Chapter 13: Archetypal Awareness	156
Poem: "Athleta Christi Nobilis"	179
Chapter 14: Coaching Archetypes	180
Poem: "Microcosm"	190
Chapter 15: The Archetype of *The Self*	192
Poem: "Insight"	205
References	208
About the Author	210
Books by Dr Elizabeth-Anne Stewart	213

Acknowledgments

My litany of gratitude extends first to the **Chicago Chapter of ICF** (*The International Coaching Federation*), which hosted my presentation on "Epiphany Moments in Coaching" during Coaching Week, 2023.
I give thanks.

***

And then to *Coaching.com* which featured "Unlocking Epiphany Moments in Coaching" in *Coaching Showcase, 2023*.
I give thanks.

***

And then to my "writing accountability partners," **Isabel Anders**, who shared so many insights and invaluable leads, and **Malcolm Tulloch**, who kept asking, *"How is the book coming along?"*
I give thanks.

***

And then to my "spirituality accountability partners,"
Evelyn Asher, Martha Bartholomew, Sr Janice Keenan, OSF, and Sr Dolores Lytle, CSA.
I give thanks.

***

And then to "The Group" from *The Institute for Life Coach Training* — **Laurie Hopkins, Rev. Rick Hastings,** and **Rev. Jim Stone**, for their supportive presence as the book unfolded.
I give thanks.

***

And then to my "Artist in Residence," **Vance J. Grant,** for his renderings and interpretations of *The Shadow*.
I give thanks.

***

And then to all my first readers and book endorsers for taking the time and for being so very kind in their comments — **Rev. Brian G. Bricker, O.P., Bill Epperly, Amy Florian, Kay Leigh Hagan, Peter A. James, Peter Metzner, DeeAnna Merz Nagel, Pat Ramcharitar,** and **Patrick Williams.**
I give thanks.

***

And then to all my "encouragers" across the globe — **friends, family, students, clients** — who understood that I had to hibernate to finish this book.
I give thanks.

***

Last but not least, thank you to the editorial team at Collective Ink for their assistance in launching *Unlocking Epiphany Moments: A Primer for Life Coaches and Other Inner Guides*.
I give thanks.

Acknowledgments

***

To all of you and to anyone whose kindness I have overlooked, please accept my heartfelt thanks!

Elizabeth

Introduction

This book has been years in the making; not in the sense that I have diligently worked on the manuscript for decades but that I have been preoccupied with the theme of *Epiphany Moments* for much of my life. *Epiphanies*, you see, involve Truth-seeking, daring to be authentic, and being open to discovery; they arise from listening to the deepest dimensions of *Self*, taking the time to reflect, and cultivating a healthy curiosity about everything. In pursuing awakening or enlightenment, I have worked with spiritual directors, therapists, coaches, and peer support groups. I have taught what I needed to learn and written what I needed to read. I have preached "to the choir," taking my own messages to heart. I have spent countless hours in silence and solitude and countless hours sharing my deepest self with trusted soul friends. In short, I have been on a quest for meaning and understanding that is so profoundly life-changing that my greatest joy is now working with those who wish to see more clearly. That, for me, is "payback," or as Joseph Campbell would say, living out of the sixth stage of *The Heroic Quest*, *The Return* — "*Return*" here meaning giving back what one has received.

But this is what we do as coaches, spiritual directors, therapists, and other inner guides. *The Call* to become professional listeners usually comes to those who have themselves grappled with painful issues and have mostly transcended them, in large part because of the focused listening of companions along the way. Because of their love, their support, and their generous attention, we have not only survived *The Road of Trials* — the third stage of *The Heroic Quest* — but have become that which we never imagined we could be, catching a glimpse of what Hinduism calls *moksha* or spiritual liberation and Buddhism names as *nirvana*. And because of our dedication to inner work, we have discovered that the path to true happiness lies not in having or doing "more" but in healthy, life-affirming detachment. It is not that we are perfect but that we have dealt with much of the baggage we once dragged through life, thereby reaching a place of calm and contentment. Letting go of our anger, resentments, and feelings of victimhood, we have learned to understand, forgive, and accept. At the same time, we have courageously extricated ourselves from destructive situations, choosing wholeness over fragmentation, life over death, the future over past happenings....

I have written this "Primer" mostly for life coaches but also for anyone who offers inner guidance, whether clergy, therapists, lay ministers, chaplains, counselors, or social workers. However, it is also a book that anyone on the path to spiritual integration should find useful. Though I myself offer both spiritual direction and life coaching, because of my involvement in coach education, coach mentoring, and global coaching communities, it made the most sense to address my comments to life coaches, keeping my content spiritual rather than religious. In my practice as an inner guide, I work primarily in Christian contexts, but also companion those from every faith tradition and those without a formal religious affiliation. My intention is to reach the broadest possible audience to maximize our contribution to planetary healing.

In terms of approaching *Unlocking Epiphany Moments: A Primer for Life Coaches and Other Inner Guides*, I suggest reading this book contemplatively. Of course, you could read it cover to cover in one sitting, but then you would miss the opportunity for reflection and integration. You could also skip the various quizzes, but then you may forgo having *Epiphany Moments* of your own. Ignoring the poems that follow each chapter would definitely speed up your reading time, but then, again, my poetry offers a window into each chapter, reinforcing each theme and allowing for a heart response.

Introduction

My hope is that this book will offer a life-changing experience rather than a series of mere facts or strategies. I send it out into the world to unblock the imagination, release creativity, deepen self-awareness, and transform consciousness — that of my readers and, just as importantly, of their clients.

Elizabeth-Anne Stewart

www.elizabeth-annestewart.com
www.MinistryCoachingFoundation.com

CHAPTER ONE

So You're Having an Epiphany Moment?

The word "Epiphany" descends from the ancient Greek "epipháneia," meaning a "manifestation or appearance." The word is built from the Greek words "pha" (to shine), "phanein" (to show, to cause to shine), and "epiphanein" (to manifest, to bring to light).

Defining *Epiphany Moments*

The term "*Epiphany*" is not a word we commonly use, nor is it one that the average educated person today may even understand. I say this not as a critique but as an observation. As language has become less formal, everyday communication tends to be simple and direct, with brevity, clarity, and immediacy prized above literary flourish. The digital age, of course, has trained all of us to be more succinct in both our written and spoken language. For example, choosing monosyllabic words over complex Greek and Latin alternatives makes all the sense in the world for someone trying to communicate via texts — and who among us has not resorted to emojis when wanting to spell out emotions?

The drawback, however, is that we have stripped language of its color, texture, and rich associations, settling for what I call "transactional interactions" — that is, ways of communicating that get to the point without acknowledging the humanity of the parties involved. This tendency began when mega stores and global franchises replaced small "mom & pop" businesses, and the butcher, baker, and candlestick maker fell into oblivion. Instead of being greeted with friendly smiles and name recognition, customers found themselves in assembly line checkouts designed to help them exit quickly.

And then, of course, came online shopping, the ultimate in depersonalization! As for other forms of communication, it is not surprising that in our fast-paced world, texting is preferable to both phone calls and emails. I have heard stories where long-distance relationships have been conducted entirely by texts, culminating in marriage proposals, also by text. Conversely, many a relationship ends with a terse text message stating the equivalent of "You're dumped!"

What is true of language can also be true of coaching. When a client and coach agree to work on specific results, goals, and outcomes to be accomplished within a specific time frame, there are expectations on both sides. The client wants results, and the coach needs to deliver them and in a collaborative relationship, this is typically what happens. However, the disadvantage of this is that when staying on track is the primary consideration, there may be missed opportunities for reflection and discovery. Take, for example, a situation in which a client hires a coach to work on weight-loss goals. Together, they develop a coaching plan, and by the end of the contract, the client now has the coveted abs and BMI. *Success!* — or is it?

Did the coach explore the *real* reasons behind the client's stated goals? Was there more behind the coaching agenda than wanting to look good and feel better? Could there have been some underlying fear about being unlovable or unacceptable? Could the client have some chronic health issues that made weight loss advisable? Was there some major life event for which the client wanted a makeover? Such questions, even if unstated, formed the subtext of their coaching agreement and to ignore them meant missing an opportunity for the client's growth and self-understanding. In other words, the client missed out on what I call *"Epiphany Moments."*

David Clutterbuck points out that when a client brings a goal to coaching, "it represents their thinking so far." In fact, because of effective coaching, the client grows in understanding, and this, in turn, causes the goal "to evolve into something different" (Clutterbuck, p. 146). *Epiphany Moments*, then, often hold an element of surprise for both coach and client; rather than hijacking the coaching agenda, they lead to deeper insights and a broader range of "next steps." In effect, such moments expand our thinking from what we have arrived at "so far" to imagining infinite possibilities.

Touching the Infinite

"Expanded thinking" might be the most we hope for in any coaching session, but the possibility of touching *The Infinite* is also there. For me, an *Epiphany Moment* goes beyond having a sudden insight or understanding a situation at a deeper level. It involves a revelation of such magnitude that our world is shaken, turned upside down, and everything we assumed we knew now seems trivial, inconsequential, and not worth mentioning. So profound is our mind shift, so revolutionary is our new way of seeing, that we are filled with awe, barely able to process the experience. Not only is language an inadequate vehicle to communicate this revelation, but even if we had the words, bringing them to speech would violate the sacredness of the moment. The minute we try to explain, define, describe, or categorize, we rob the experience of its mystery. Instead of basking in awe and wonder, we suddenly feel illiterate, especially when the response amounts to blank stares and puzzled frowns.

Take Plato's *Allegory of the Cave*. Set as a dialogue between Socrates and Plato's brother, Glaukon, the allegory begins with a description of chained captives whose only view of reality since birth is a succession of shadows on a cave wall. "But just suppose," posits Socrates, "that one of the captives is dragged up the steep incline out of the cavern and firmly held until at last he stands in the light of the sun." Gradually, this captive adjusts to the blinding light until he not only sees things "as they are" but can also behold the heavenly bodies. His *Epiphany*, if you will, is that he has merely existed in a cave of shadows, in an unreal world that masqueraded as reality. To return to such a world would be a cruel fate indeed, but perhaps the worst horror of all would be the disbelief of his fellow captives. For them, he would be a laughing stock; one whose adventures into the sunshine have ruined his capacity to see as they see.

Examples of Epiphany Moments

With a background in spirituality/ theology/ literature, it is not surprising that I gravitate towards *Epiphanies*. Like many people, my first exposure to the term came from celebrating the *Feast of the Epiphany*, the Christian feast commemorating the visit of the Magi to the humble birthplace of the Child Jesus in Bethlehem. According to tradition (Matthew 2:1–12), astronomers from the East observed astrological phenomena that indicated the birth of a mighty ruler. Moreover, since prophetic texts supported their celestial observations, they went in search of the newborn king to pay him homage. What they found, in the glory of straw, was the Holy Child, the Star of Jacob. In effect, they witnessed a manifestation of the Divine — a theophany! But to experience this life-changing moment of illumination, the Magi had to leave their comfort zones. Armed with their research and calculations, they embarked on a hazardous journey from the known to the unknown, guided by the light of that one star. Stiff from the saddle, weary of desert storms, bored by the incessant jangle of camel harnesses, they made their way across hostile terrain, risking their lives for the sake of the enlightenment they were seeking. Such a journey cannot be taken virtually, nor is it an adventure to be lived vicariously — to arrive somewhere one is meant to be demands nothing short of "everything." And then, of course, there is the question of the return. Having bypassed the court of the wicked king who was intent on murdering the Holy Child, the Magi then had another long journey ahead of them. This time there was no heavenly star to illumine the way, but we can assume that an inner light led them safely home, away from court intrigues and nefarious plots.

On a personal level, I feel very connected to this Infancy Narrative from *The Gospel of St. Matthew*. It was on 5 January 1973 that, having boxed up my possessions and having packed the largest suitcase I could find, I left my Mediterranean home, the island of Malta, with a brand-new BA (Hons) in English, as the "souvenir" bride of a Peace Corps volunteer. Arriving in Chicago the next day — the *Feast of the Epiphany* — to sub-zero temperatures, I experienced instant culture shock and acute homesickness, both exacerbated by the knowledge that there was no going back, even if I wanted to. At the same time, however, I sensed that, like the Magi, I was on a journey of spiritual and intellectual discovery; somehow, their story was my story. That thought was comforting, especially in those dark, dark moments when my star seemed to have vanished or at least lost its brilliance...

Blocks to Star Quests

Not everyone can find their star, let alone follow it; few even know that such a star exists, and not many even care... Sadly, the pressures of society and the hardships that come our way can block our view of the heavens, clouding our belief in possibility or even in a divinely governed universe. Weighed down by the pressures of daily life, we no longer behold the stars, let alone see our unique star. Instead, our consciousness is clouded, not only by the toxicity we take in from our environment but also by the negative thoughts that originate within. On the one hand there is the endless barrage of "bad news," whether it be wars, natural disasters, political shenanigans, or horrific crimes against humanity. On the other, there are our negative assumptions about life — *"Something bad is about to happen!"*; *"It's dangerous to be in crowds"*; *"If COVID doesn't get us, some other disease will"; "The economy is about to crash"; "There's no point making any effort as it won't get us anywhere"; "Nothing good ever comes my way"; "Don't trust anyone"; "If I don't do the job it won't get done"; "It's best to leave things as they are or we risk failing..."*

This toxic mix robs us of our creativity and courage, reducing us to victims who "live and partly live" instead of being *"Heroes"* who embrace life in its fullness. Unable to see in the dark, we focus, instead, on surviving and getting by. Life becomes static, boring, and rote. Losing sight of our extraordinary potential for greatness, we waste countless hours surfing the net, engaging with social media, shopping online, watching TV, or deadening our brains in myriad ways — in other words, in what I call "statistical living."

W. H. Auden, the twentieth-century English poet, describes one version of such a life in his poem, *The Unknown Citizen*. His subject is an exemplary citizen who works in a factory, goes to war when drafted, pays his dues, causes no disturbances, marries on time, produces children on time, pays for his appliances on time, holds the right opinions, reads the daily newspaper and is appropriately insured. The poem concludes with the following lines: *"Was he free? Was he happy? The question is absurd: Had anything been wrong, we should certainly have heard."* Auden's nameless individual has learned to conform to society's expectations but has ceased to wonder, to dream, or to go in search of his star. Instead, he has led an "unexamined life," following neon lights instead of heavenly lights, content to stay home instead of taking off on adventures, and always letting others dictate how he should spend his time. Now, here I'm going beyond Auden's text and indulging some assumptions of my own. I see this *Unknown Citizen* as a representative of unconscious living. If he is religious, this is more of a cultural commitment than a love affair with the *Holy One*: he crosses himself, recites the prayers, receives the sacraments, but keeps God at a safe distance. Meanwhile, his star twinkles brightly overhead, unobserved, while the holy place to which it points remains devoid of visitors.

Divine Breakthroughs

What wisdom might the holy travelers — the Magi — wish to share with the *Unknown Citizen*? I suspect they would encourage him to look beyond the material universe to discover where Mystery is inviting him. They would urge him to leave behind his comfort zones and to travel where Light beckons, embracing his own unique journey. And they would assure him that the star assigned to him at birth will guide him to wherever he is meant to be, no matter how far he must travel. It is the one journey that matters....

There are other moments of revelation in the Christian scriptures, for example, the Baptism of Jesus and the Transfiguration. However, *Epiphanies* are to be found in all religions: Moses taking off his shoes before the Burning Bush (Judaism); the Infant Buddha taking seven steps at birth and proclaiming, "I alone am the world-honored one" (Buddhism); Arjuna beholding all gods in Krishna, the god serving as his charioteer in the *Bhagavad Gita* (Hinduism); Mohammed's night journey from the Great Mosque in Mecca to the Temple Mount in Jerusalem (Islam), and so forth. These and other stories allow the Divine to break into human reality. Amid darkness, Holy Light scatters shards of hope, reminding worshippers that Light is stronger than despair, that good will overcome evil, and that Death is not the final word. *Epiphanies* allow us to catch a glimpse of heaven on earth, to connect with our *Divine Source*, and to remember, as Teilhard de Chardin so aptly said, "We are not human beings having a spiritual experience; we are spiritual beings having a human experience."

Aristotle and Epiphany Moments

The world of literature is also replete with *Epiphanies*. Aristotle, in his *Ars Poetica*, defines *Epiphany Moments* as "a change from ignorance to knowledge, and it leads either to love or to hatred between persons destined for good or ill fortune" (*Classical Literary Criticism*, 46). In coaching, of course, it is the first part of this definition that is the best fit. Ideally, at the end of a single session or by the end of the contracted time, the client has experienced such a powerful "mind shift" that returning to old ways and beliefs is impossible; but, as Aristotle points out, some discoveries are better than others.

At the bottom of the list are discoveries made by "visible signs and tokens"; these, according to Aristotle, lack invention and artistry. A coaching example might be a client who decides to pursue a specific career because an owl happened to perch on the windowsill or because an unusual pattern of tea leaves formed at the bottom of a teacup. Now, though we might dismiss such "signs" as mere superstition, people tend to find meaning in signs, along with a sense of direction — and sometimes signs have altered the course of history. Eusebius of Caesarea, in his *Vita Constantini,* records Constantine's vision of an emblem of Christ in the sky, which was accompanied by the words, "In this sign you will conquer."

Amazed at the spectacle, Constantine and his army placed the sign on their shields before engaging in battle. Following his victory and accession as Emperor, Constantine reinstated religious freedom, restored confiscated property to Christians, and, in effect, became the Church's patron. Some Church histories go as far as to claim that because of this vision, the Church of Martyrs became the Church of the Establishment.

Then come *Epiphany Moments* "manufactured by the poet and which are inartistic for that reason." To illustrate this, Aristotle uses an example from Euripides' play, *Iphigenia in Tauris*. Right before Iphigenia is about to sacrifice Orestes and his friend,

Pylades, in Artemis' temple, the brother and sister recognize each other just in time. Though Iphigenia feels a connection to these strangers who hail from her home city of Argos, it is a letter that finally reveals that Orestes is actually her brother.

"Take this letter to Orestes and let him know Iphigenia lives," says Iphigenia to Pylades, who is standing next to Orestes.

"Orestes, here is a letter from your sister," says Plyades to Orestes, handing him the tablets.

For Aristotle, this moment of discovery is contrived rather than organic; it is a little too clever and offers the protagonists a last-minute reprieve rather than a well-earned escape. In coaching, this might translate to clients being told "the Truth" rather than discovering it themselves. When a coach asks leading questions or pushes the client in a specific direction, the client loses autonomy, and the coach drives the process.

If the coach or inner guide is going to be directive, there needs to be a compelling reason for this — and, occasionally, there is. Many years ago, when I was serving as a university minister at a Catholic university, one of the students was infatuated with a male colleague of mine who happened to be gay. So obsessed was this student that she would "do the daily rounds" of all the campus ministry offices, sharing her tears and story of rejection with one minister after another. My colleague was strikingly handsome, funny, and compassionate, so I could understand the attraction; however, "Eddie" soon began to feel harassed. The more he withdrew, the more desperate "Amy" became.

Finally, I felt an intervention was necessary. Having spent several hours weeping in different offices, Amy knocked on my door. I should specify here that I was not seeing her for guidance, but she would stop by to chat with regularity. As usual, the conversation began with tears.

"I don't understand why he rejects me!" Amy sobbed. "Why am I so unlovable?"

For a minute, I was silent. Then, I chose my words carefully.

"Suppose it's not you who is the problem, Amy. Suppose Eddie's feelings towards you have nothing to do with your being unlovable."

Amy looked up at me in surprise, her face contorted in a frown.

"If you can believe you are lovable, why might Eddie not respond to you?" I continued.

"Because he's in love with someone else?" asked Amy, looking devastated at this possibility.

"Maybe," I said. "But what other reasons might there be?"

"Perhaps he's still getting over a broken relationship?" suggested Amy, looking more hopeful.

"Maybe," I said, "but what else can you come up with?"

"No — he's not..."

"Not what, Amy?"

"I think I understand," she said, getting up to leave. Though I was "directive" in this situation, my intervention ended this unrequited love saga without Eddie having to "come out" to a student and without my doing anything more than asking a few simple questions. Again, I want to stress that I was not seeing "Amy" for any form of inner guidance; I was simply a chaplain on call.

A third kind of discovery is "due to memory when the sight of something leads to the required understanding." Personally, I would imagine that any sensory experience can jolt memory, not just sight. For example, the aroma of chestnuts roasting on an open fire might trigger memories of Christmases past, while the scent of "Old Spice Classic" might re-awaken memories of one's grandfather or great-grandfather.

Once, during a creative writing class, a student brought in an old, stained hat about which he wanted to write.

"No, it's not mine," he said, "but it belongs to someone I knew and could have saved..."

Intrigued, we listened as he described going into a restaurant with pockets stuffed with $20 bills, his "take" after betting on a college football game. As he proceeded to order the most expensive items on the menu, he noticed a shabbily dressed man at an adjacent table. At first, he didn't pay much attention to this individual, but then it became clear that whatever the student ordered, the man also ordered. Finally, it came time to pay. The student pulled out wads of bills, leaving a generous tip; the other man stood up and tried to leave without paying.

Several wait staff and the manager blocked the man from leaving, and seeing a scuffle ensuing, the student exited as quickly as possible. He had barely closed the door behind him when there were deafening screams and the sound of shattering glass. There, spreadeagled in a pool of blood on the sidewalk, was his dining companion. Stunned, the student picked up the man's hat to give it to him, but it was clear the man would not be needing it. By the time the ambulance arrived, he was already dead.

"I could have saved him," explained the student. "I had the money and could have paid for his meal. That's why I kept his hat…"

That tragic encounter was life-changing; the student kept the hat as a reminder to help those who crossed his path in whatever way he could. Moreover, by sharing his stories with others — including our class — he hoped to inspire his audience to be attentive to those in need.

The fourth kind of *Epiphany* is "the result of reasoning" or deduction: since xxx happened, xxx must be true. Aristotle conveniently provides this example: "Someone who is like me has come; no one is like me except Orestes; therefore, it is Orestes who has come." I imagine a coaching conversation that goes something like this:

COACH: "So why are you so sure you will be laid off?"

CLIENT: "The company is going to lay off the most recent hires. I was hired this year. All my team members were hired last year; therefore, I am the team member who will be laid off."

Or like this:

COACH: "So what makes you so sure your boss will know you reported the defective elevator?"

CLIENT: "The complaint referred to poor maintenance on the 'lift.' I am the only person in the office to use British terminology — anyone else would have said, 'elevator' — therefore, everyone will know that I was the whistleblower."

Obviously, a *real* coaching conversation wouldn't sound so stilted or be so devoid of emotion, but the use of reasoning can lead to new awareness or provide clarity, especially with clients who tend to be cerebral.

And finally, the highest form of *Epiphany* is when startling disclosures emerge organically from probable events, as in the case of Oedipus, who discovers that he inadvertently murdered his father, married his mother, and fathered his siblings. Aristotle concludes that this type of revelation, which emerges from the events themselves, is infinitely superior to those that depend upon "such artificial aids as tokens and necklaces." Unlike the recognition scene in Euripides' *Iphigenia in Tauris*, Oedipus' mind-shattering discovery is woven, thread by thread, throughout the fabric of the play, gradually preparing the audience for the revelations to come.

Revelation was not only a standard feature of classical drama but also influenced the literature that followed. Shakespeare, for example, was the master of "organic *Epiphanies*." In *Othello*, the protagonist is driven to murderous envy by his evil captain, Iago. Too late, he discovers that Iago has fabricated evidence of Desdemona's infidelity and that he, Othello, has killed his virtuous wife because of his subordinate's trickery. In another tragedy, *King Lear*, the king experiences a series of *Epiphanies* around his folly in dividing his kingdom between the two heartless daughters who flattered him while he banished Cordelia, the daughter who truly loved him. The pain of these revelations is enough to drive him mad — a reminder that too much clarity delivered too quickly can cause a psychotic break!

Revelation in Fiction

As a genre, the short story depends upon *Epiphany Moments*. The action begins with the *status quo* and then builds on a series of setbacks, challenges, and reversals toward the climax; what follows is the denouement when the strands of the plot are brought together, and that which was hidden is now in plain view. Not only does the protagonist experience an *Epiphany*, but the minor characters and even the reader experience new insight. In Flannery O'Connor's *Revelation*, Mrs Turpin prides herself on being an upright Christian woman whom Jesus has blessed with superior gifts. Set in a doctor's waiting room, the story demonstrates Mrs Turpin's smug piety as she condescendingly views the "trashy people" waiting with her while she silently thanks Jesus for making her just the way she is.

Unexpectedly, an ugly girl with acne and piercing eyes hurls her book at Mrs Turpin, catching her under the left eye before letting out a bloodcurdling howl and sinking her fingers into the woman's neck. Mary Grace, it seems, can read Mrs Turpin's thoughts and, driven into a frenzy by her hypocrisy, screams, "Go back to hell where you came from, you old wart hog!" Later, pondering over these words near her pristine pig parlor, Mrs Turpin has a disturbing vision: there, in the visionary light, she sees a vast horde of souls rumbling towards heaven — an assembly of trash, freaks, and lunatics — and there, bringing up the rear, are people just like Mrs Turpin and her husband, Claud, who have always had "a little of everything and the God-given wit to use it right."

Epiphany Moments in Coaching

And so back to coaching. The same types of *Epiphanies* that we encounter in religion and literature also surface in coaching. The client comes in with an agenda, and if the coach pays close attention and listens for the subtexts, "something more" will surface. During the coaching conversation, the client often indicates the real agenda through facial expressions, body language, and word choices. This "something more" might involve a happy discovery, a new sense of direction, and an experience of hope and possibility; conversely, it might lead a client to acknowledge deep-rooted character flaws, inappropriate behaviors, and self-sabotaging attitudes. The coach's task is neither to censor the emerging *Epiphany* nor to fabricate a favorable discovery; rather, the coach serves the client by serving the Truth, even when the revelation may be unwelcome. In my experience, however, the benefits always outweigh the pain, and the *Epiphany Moment* becomes an invaluable catalyst for change.

Let's imagine a coaching client who is trying to discern whether to retire at 62 or wait until 70 to receive a higher monthly Social Security benefit. First, the coaching conversation revolves entirely around finances, with the client comparing the pros and cons of each option. The focus mostly concerns the cost of living, projected expenses, and the lifestyle changes that would come with early retirement. The coach meanwhile senses a heaviness to the conversation, noting that the client has little energy or enthusiasm. "I'm just wondering how you FEEL about retiring," observes the coach. With this statement, the conversation takes an entirely different direction. It turns out that the real issue is not financial but one of self-identity: who will the client BE without a job title, job description, and direct reports? With this *Epiphany*, **real** coaching can begin.

But how do you know if you — or your client — are having an *Epiphany*? If you are intuitive, you will feel it and know it in your bones, so to speak. The American poet, Emily Dickinson, once remarked in a letter that "If I read a book [and] ... feel physically as if the top of my head were taken off, I know that is poetry." Physical reactions accompany *Epiphany Moments* just as they accompany poetry. We know we are experiencing such a moment when there is a thrill of recognition, a shudder of shock, a wave of warmth, or a chilly sensation gravitating down the spine.... Reactions will vary depending upon the type of *Epiphany*. If there has been some kind of spiritual awakening or manifestation of *The Holy*, coach and client may experience a sense of awe. On the other hand, if the client suddenly has some humorous insight, then both coach and client may laugh with unrestrained relief. Conversely, if the client moves beyond scapegoating others and finally accepts personal blame for a situation, then an icy chill may be the response.

An observant coach is also attuned to shifts in emotions. The advantage of *seeing* the client (as opposed to a phone session) is that the coach can observe shifts in body language and facial expression. Such clues indicate that "something" is taking place internally — perhaps the client is finally at peace over a painful decision, suddenly sees new previously invisible options, or is filled with gratitude....

On the other hand, some coaches find that working with clients via conference call, without video, allows them to listen more deeply to what is being said. Without visual distractions, they can pay better attention to the client's tone of voice, word choices, and emotional shifts. Just as someone who loses physical sight learns to compensate by relying on heightened auditory abilities, so coaches who rely on listening skills may hear more deeply than those of us who prefer an audio-visual coaching approach.

Either way, *Epiphany Moments* are extraordinary, which is why we know when they are happening. They carry us out of the realm of the ordinary into clarity and insight, functioning as prophetic guides that bring invitations, affirmations, warnings, and reprimands. No matter what their message is, they demand attention.

SUMMARY

- *Epiphany Moments* are moments of manifestation, insight, revelation, and discovery.
- They often lead to profound emotions.
- They occur in religion, literature, and every aspect of life.
- They shatter assumptions, self-deception, and ignorance.
- They can lead to mind shifting and new directions.
- They reveal the best and worst things about us.
- In coaching, they invite the client to move beyond the stated agenda into deeper but related territory.
- *Epiphany Moments* are often accompanied by physical sensations.

"Reality"

"Reality," Eliot would say,
"is too much for humankind."
Now, I know what he meant:
When all things are in focus,
Sharply delineated,
Freed from shadows,
When one's ears are unstopped
And one's cataracts removed,
Then the knife
Twists in the soul
Bringing deeper clarity still
Like too much sun
On a ski-slope
Or intense light
After anesthesia.
Dark glasses lost,
I perceive how others
Avoid my burning gaze
As though afraid
Of what I might reveal,
Afraid, too, of the contagion
That rawness brings

***

When there is too much
to bear.

***

Woman Dreamer, 1989

CHAPTER TWO

Archimedes Takes a Bath!

The "Eureka!" Legend

According to the writings of Roman historian, Marcus Vitruvius Pollio, King Hiero II, the Greek tyrant of Syracuse (c.308–215 BCE), enlisted Archimedes' help when he suspected a craftsman had substituted cheap metal for gold in his new crown. This was no ordinary crown but was fashioned in the shape of a laurel wreath to symbolize the king's military victories. Moreover, it was destined to be a votive offering in gratitude to the gods — in other words, by donating the crown, the king would be fulfilling a solemn vow. Despite the crown's great beauty, rumors began to surface about the quality of the gold — and, by extension, about the quality of King Hiero's votive offering.

Archimedes is said to have wrestled with his assignment for days, which was by then a matter of high national importance; both the king's honor and the favor of the gods were at stake. Fortunately, there was a happy ending to this fanciful tale. Vitruvius claims that Archimedes found his answer while bathing. Noting how much water he himself displaced, he suddenly realized that if an object is completely submerged, it displaces the same volume of fluid as the volume of the object. That's when he reputedly shouted *"Eureka! Eureka!"* and jumped out of the bath, running naked through the streets of Syracuse. Putting his displacement principle to the test, he submerged both the crown and a lump of gold that supposedly weighed the same; since the crown displaced less water than the gold, he concluded the king had been defrauded.

Though I have simplified the various steps in Archimedes' experiment, I hope I have retained the power of his "Eureka!"

experience — *"I've found it!"* In his jubilation, Archimedes was too overwhelmed to realize he had forgotten to dress; in his moment of brilliance, he babbled like a madman as he rushed to conduct his experiment. Fact or fiction, the story illustrates the profound effect that an *Epiphany Moment* can have on the recipient and its life-changing consequences. Here is a breakdown of events:

- King Hiero suspects he has been cheated.
- This is more than a monetary issue but reflects the king's "brand" and how he relates to the gods.
- King Hiero summons Archimedes and orders him to get to the bottom of the matter.
- This is more than a monetary issue; it reflects Archimedes' "brand" and how he relates to the king.
- At the same time, a human life is at stake: that of the craftsman. If Archimedes comes to the wrong conclusion, an innocent man could end up in the torturer's chamber — or a guilty man could escape all punishment. In effect, Archimedes is to be both judge and executioner.
- Faced with an impossible task, Archimedes takes "time out" in the bathtub.
- While he is relaxing, a new scientific principle breaks through his consciousness, seemingly from nowhere.
- Archimedes is so awe-struck that he leaps out of the bath, focused only on this momentous discovery.
- Now, he can turn to science to find the definitive answer to ensure justice is done.

Information Gaps

Many of the elements in this summary apply to *Epiphany Moments* in general. In the first place, there is a situation of "unknowing" in which the key players are seeking the truth. For Archimedes and the king, there are only two options: the craftsman is either innocent or guilty. In the case of ourselves or our clients, we may be oblivious to the fact that we don't know something, or we may be painfully aware that there is a gap in our knowledge.

Secondly, not knowing tends to be a liability. Both King Hiero and Archimedes have their reputations to protect. Similarly, we and our clients cannot function at our full potential or make informed decisions when we lack information or, worse still, when we have the wrong information. When we are aware of a knowledge gap, we can drive ourselves into a frenzy trying to arrive at the knowledge we need. This is especially true when our decisions depend upon knowing if something is — or is not — going to happen. For example, last summer I reluctantly agreed to teach an undergraduate course because without knowing whether a program I directed would continue to have institutional support, I needed to ensure I had some income. That proved to be the right decision. However, I then accepted two more courses for the fall just in case a new venture I had launched failed to receive the much-desired ICF accreditation. In this instance, my inability to live with uncertainty made me overextend myself when I should have invested my energy in my own programming. Very often, in coaching contexts, a client will require help sorting through various options, each of which may depend upon a specific piece of information that is presently unavailable. Even more complicated are those scenarios when we — or our clients — don't know that we don't know. Sometimes, there may be information that never reached us or that we failed to register. Perhaps we planned a last-minute vacation without checking whether heatwaves, hurricanes, or floods were likely to impact our trip. Or we went ahead with an expensive purchase without knowing that our position could be eliminated in a company merger. Or we invested in a friend's business without first checking to see his or her success or failure track record. Or perhaps we went ahead with relocating away from family to a distant state because we were unaware that a close relative was terminally ill.

"If only I had known" becomes a refrain of regret when we realize our decisions were based on not knowing. But "not knowing" is not just about decision-making. In coaching and other forms of inner guidance, clients can suddenly take ownership of less-than-admirable attitudes and behaviors. Conversely, clients may suddenly recognize that it is neither fate nor bad luck that is sabotaging their careers but their unwillingness to take risks, their lack of imagination, their refusal to delegate.

Then, again, clients may suddenly grasp their amazing potential and that they have what it takes to accept leadership positions, not only at a local level but even globally! Such discoveries are the equivalent of Archimedes' "Eureka!" moment; they leave us in fear, trembling, amazement, awe, and disbelief. In a moment, the world as we know it is turned upside down, and we find ourselves gazing into a mirror that either illuminates everything we need to know or helps us recognize all the distortions that shaped our prior thinking. It is as if the gods — or God — have suddenly stripped away everything that veiled our consciousness.

Silence, Solitude, and Rest

Epiphany Moments seldom "just happen." Like Archimedes, we need to wrestle with the information gap until we exhaust all options. Then, when the rational mind fails to provide the answers we need, taking a bath, going for a run, or resorting to some other contemplative practice opens us up to receptivity. Silence, solitude, and rest, in fact, are three essential conditions for enlightenment. In their absence "monkey mind" — that phenomenon of the racing mind — leads us away from clarity into a confusing maze of jumbled thoughts, feelings, and associations.

Meditation teachers advise novices to ignore the images that flit across the screens of their minds or simply to observe them, without judgment. This is sound advice for meditation, but the modern mind seldom pauses to meditate and instead races without cessation, jumping from one thought to the next. *What's next on my calendar? Will my client show up? Have I overdrawn my bank account? Will I have time to get to the post office? What's for supper? Who will pick up the kids? Should I hand in my notice? Is this indigestion or a heart attack? Has someone hacked my email account? Should I head home or go to the gym? Why can't I lose weight? I wonder what s/he is doing right now? Should I call or wait for them to call me? I wonder who sent her flowers? I hope I won't go bald like my dad! I wonder if Mum is feeling better today...*

Such ponderings stress us out, preoccupying us as different scenarios play in our heads, raising our cortisol levels (and our blood pressure!) and depleting both our energy and our creativity. We seek relief by plugging into a music playlist, or the news, or social media, trying to drown out all the troublesome thoughts with a different kind of noise, or else starting a chat — in person or virtual — to distract us. Meanwhile, inspiration passes us by, and The Muse graces someone with a quieter, more reflective mind.

For many, being alone, even for a short period of time, is terrifying, and so they turn to constant texting or using FaceTime to alleviate anxiety temporarily. This is why losing a mobile phone — or, in the case of teenagers, having it confiscated — can be so devastating. The mobile has become a lifeline for those who always need connectivity to others. If, for some reason, a friend or loved one fails to answer, then the caller desperately tries the next person on the list, and the next after that, until someone finally does respond. That failing, there is always Amazon's "Alexa" to fill the communication gap and create the illusion of companionship. Illusions and epiphanies, however, are mutually exclusive, and the more we engage in meaningless chatter, the less likely we are to listen to the voice within, that guiding voice that opens us up to new dimensions of reality, if we would only listen.

"Dreams do not come/ when one resists the message/ or persists in stubbornness," I wrote in "Fish Song" (*Woman Dreamer*, 1989). In this poem, a female Jonah acknowledges that it was fear that entangled her, binding her feet, numbing her heart, until she no longer heard the Word within. If fear is the greatest block to awareness, then surrender to Truth ultimately helps us see. If we cling to our take on reality, *Epiphanies* are unlikely to happen; however, when we cultivate "mindfulness" through silence, solitude, and rest, we open ourselves to the gift of awareness.

In *The Miracle of Mindfulness*, Thich Nhat Hanh illustrates how we can wake up to life through simple practices such as "washing the dishes to wash the dishes" instead of treating washing dishes as a dreaded chore. Or savoring every aspect of a tangerine from the color of its skin to its aromatic zest. He also teaches that the most important moment is NOW, that the most important person is the one we are presently with, and that our most important task is to make that person happy. If we practice mindfulness, we clear our minds of clutter and open our hearts to insight, mystery, and transformation.

Mindfulness is also the perfect antidote to trying to control *Epiphany Moments*. Because it grounds us in the present, it keeps us from anticipating the future and dwelling on the past. Living in the present only, we become more humble, more accepting, more grateful for the life we are living. Strange as it may seem, some believe they can summon *Epiphanies* at whim, on their own terms. Many years ago, a seminarian came to see me after experiencing a powerful theophany in the school chapel. His experience, it turned out, was multi-faceted. After listening to his description of an overwhelmingly powerful experience of God's Presence, I asked him how he had responded.

"I took a shower," he said.

"A shower?"

"Yes, to wash it off."

"I'm sorry—"

"A cold shower. The feeling was so terrifying I wanted no part of it."

Not surprisingly, the seminarian didn't have an adequate vocabulary to describe what had happened; the experience was simply too extraordinary, and words were inadequate. Then, his mood shifted.

"But I'm pretty frustrated," he went on. "I've gone back to the chapel at the same time every day and waited for it to happen again. It hasn't."

"But didn't you try washing it off?" I countered.

"Yes, but God should know I wasn't ready then, but I am now. I've shown up multiple times, and he's not responding. Quite honestly, I'm beginning to doubt if there is a God — I'm seeking but not finding, knocking on the door, and there's no answer."

There was a period of awkward silence as I tried to make sense of what I'd just heard.

"Perhaps we could focus on what the experience was trying to teach you," I said. "Why did it come to you at that precise time in your life, and what did it want of you? How can you best respond now?"

I don't believe we got very far.

SUMMARY

- *Epiphany Moments* begin with "unknowing"; we are either aware of an information gap or oblivious to its existence.
- Not knowing tends to be a liability, especially when important decisions are involved.

- Sometimes, we and our clients are unaware that we don't know; we cling to our assumptions and the lies we have told ourselves, often because of fear.
- When there is a breakthrough in consciousness, we can be startled into a new experience of reality.
- We cannot force *Epiphany Moments* to happen, but we can be receptive to them, especially through contemplative practice and surrender to Truth.
- Three essential qualities for welcoming *Epiphanies* are silence, solitude, and rest.
- The practice of mindfulness helps us to declutter our tired brains; it also protects us from becoming too attached to our *Epiphany Moments*.

"Primeval"

In that time,
In that sacred time,
When we spoke like gods
And walked with them
At eventide,
In that time,
In that sacred time,
When we battled darkness
With swords of burnished gold
And danced to make
The spring rains fall,
Then, in that sacred place,
We knew the necessary magic
To protect, ensnare,
Heal and multiply
All living things.
Now, around dim flames,
We grope for words
To describe
Our fractured memories
And stir up embers
For forgotten syllables
Of power.

Frost and Fire, 1985

CHAPTER THREE

Blocks to Epiphany Moments

Maintaining the Status Quo

It is hard to imagine that clients would seek out coaching or inner guidance of any kind unless they were open to learning the Truth about themselves, others, or the situations in which they find themselves. Surprisingly, learning the Truth is probably not high on most people's agenda. In my experience, clients often show up wanting their worldview reinforced and affirmed, hoping to identify the "next steps" that will help them maintain the *status quo* or learn how to operate within it. For many clients, security tends to be more important than Truth-seeking. They would rather learn to fit in than explore what they *really* want to do. They prefer to achieve recognition within the system than to risk venturing out on their own and they are all too willing to accept others' expectations and to ignore healthier or happier options for themselves. In effect, many clients want to be listened to but don't necessarily listen in turn. They crave the undivided attention they receive — that sense of positive regard — but don't want their beliefs and assumptions to be punctured. The implied formula goes something like this:

I will pay you to accept me unconditionally, listen with undivided attention, and help me feel better about myself than I did at the beginning of our session. You will recognize my brilliance and help me identify the steps I need to take to maintain my world.

My main objection to such a formula is that it reduces coaching to a "show and tell" session, offering little room for discovery — and no room for life-transforming *Epiphanies*! Instead of providing an opening for revelation, it keeps the conversation safe, with the coach's "hmms" simply reinforcing the client's worldview. Instead of inviting a three-way exchange between coach, client, and *Mystery* (the unknown), it can degenerate into a monologue with an audience of one (the coach).

As coaches, we can be lulled into listening to our clients' lengthy narratives. Their stories engage us — especially if they reflect frustration, disappointment, sadness, or loss. Empathic by nature, we coaches make great passive listeners, taking in all that our clients present, often forgetting that there are multiple ways of telling any story — and multiple viewpoints! Because we genuinely care for our clients, we believe their version of events, often losing all objectivity as we express concern, sympathy, and even outrage. Not wanting to interrupt their narratives, we say little but communicate our attention through our body language, steady eye contact, and vocalizations. Then, when the session's close approaches, we commiserate with them and focus on "next steps" that will bring some relief.

Holistic Coaching

But as you will most likely agree, coaching is *not* a passive activity. Rather, we are called to bring our whole selves to the coaching engagement, not only listening with our hearts but also with our heads. Fully attentive to everything the client is saying, we note what is being triggered in us and what memories and experiences suggest an alternative interpretation of events. Observing the client, we listen carefully for tone of voice, imagery, word choices, and other clues to deeper meaning.

As the narrative becomes more complicated and the telling gains momentum, we invite the client to pause for a few minutes of silent reflection. In those brief moments of "time out," we examine our thoughts and feelings, waiting for any questions that may surface in the waiting. Then we continue to listen, but now with greater objectivity. Instead of endorsing the client's interpretation of events, we can play the devil's advocate, asking those essential "what if" questions that puncture the narrative, making *Epiphany Moments* possible:

What if your colleague *were* telling the truth and really was ill that day?

- What if the server went down during that online meeting and someone was not trying to sabotage the event?
- What if the person you intend to fire is the only employee who understands how to run the company?
- What if your frequent absences are causing the morale problem?
- What if you delegated some of your responsibilities to your direct reports?
- What if you could take a vacation?
- What if you were to speak to your manager about this?
- What if you were to start your own business?
- What if you could invest in new software?
- What if you were to host the next department meeting?
- What if *you* could set the ground rules?

When we move away from endorsing everything the client says to asking provocative questions, we begin to dismantle blocks to insight and new thinking. "What if?" interrupts the client's well-rehearsed monologue — perhaps a monologue that has been shared countless times with various sympathetic audiences. Though you, as coach, might be hearing the story for the first time, the client has no doubt shared it so many times that it has taken on a life of its own, with various additions and deletions re-writing the script to the client's advantage. Now, I'm not suggesting that clients lie intentionally; rather, the stories we tell have a habit of morphing from the original "facts" to more embellished versions that portray us as "more sinned against than sinning," to quote King Lear.

Probing Deeper

Whenever we cling to embellished stories, we convince ourselves that events happened in the way we describe them. "I got laid off because my supervisor was sexist" sounds better than "I was let go because I couldn't keep up with technology changes." Similarly, "I botched the interview because I was up with a sick child all night" evokes more sympathy than admitting, "I botched the job interview because I had one too many drinks the night before." But while embellishing stories is as old as humanity, our task as coaches is not merely to listen to the surface layer but to probe deeper — to excavate, if you will, beneath the various embellishments to the core meaning. An archaeological dig provides a helpful metaphor for narrative coaching. As a teenager, I often spent Saturdays excavating Punic tombs with classmates from my convent boarding school along with our peers from a nearby boys' college. Under the expert tutelage of Fr George, we would gather on-site while he surveyed the land. The terrain was rocky, crisscrossed with what archaeologists at that time believed were ancient cart ruts. Silently, we waited while Fr George explained various geological features; then, when he said "Dig!" we dug. It was uncanny how he knew where the tombs were located and how he calculated precisely how much topsoil we could shovel away before having to proceed with greater caution. Eventually, spades gave way to hand shovels, digging to scraping. Then, as the tomb shaft appeared, all work would stop. Stepping back, we watched in awe as Fr George and one or two others from the group gently removed loose soil and debris, revealing an urn, a complete amphora, some pottery shards, and an oil lamp. To our disappointment, once Fr George had identified the location and contents of a tomb, that was precisely when he instructed us to cover it up again.

"What about the urn and the amphora?" we asked. "And what about the oil lamp?"

I don't remember that he ever told us the urn contained cremated human remains dating from somewhere between the first and fourth centuries BCE. He did, however, explain that further excavations would be up to the National Museum and that every object would have to be left in situ so specialists could interpret its placement and relationship to other artifacts. Where archaeology was concerned, it seemed that the value of an artifact lay in its cultural context — in what it revealed about the customs, beliefs, rituals, and way of life of the civilization that produced it.

So, too, with "coaching artifacts." Gradually, proceeding with care and reverence, the skilled coach excavates various layers of meaning, starting with the topsoil and moving slowly through deeper layers to reach that which is buried — if the client is ready for this! Then, all being well, coach and client can explore the context of each new revelation.

Identifying Coaching Artifacts

Assuming our coaching approach is successful, what might we discover? Underlying the desire to preserve the *status quo* and maintain embellished stories, there is usually one prime artifact: Fear. Fear, of course, takes many forms. There is fear of failure, fear of success, fear of what others might think, and fear of the self we must face in the mirror. For those who have carefully cultivated a public *persona* designed to impress or intimidate, the *"Who am I really?"* question can be terrifying. In our consumer society, "success" not only depends upon marketing goods and services, but also on creating our own unique brand that will set us apart from the competition by bestowing "influencer" status. In effect, we market ourselves by flaunting everything about ourselves, from what we wear to where we live, from what we own to where we vacation. Every post on social media — even our "likes" — basically reinforces our brand. While this can be done tastefully and in moderation, self-branding can become an obsession, taking on a life of its own that is so multi-layered that we lose all sense of the self beneath the externals. In effect, we identify so strongly with the brand that we forget what it is like to be "me."

Worse still, others respond to the *"persona"* we present publicly, imagining that this *persona* is who we really are; this, in turn, reinforces the need to keep up appearances and exceed expectations. Our "brand," then, completely takes over our lives, and we feel compelled to reinforce it in any way possible. This can lead to living beyond our means, taking personal risks, and even jeopardizing our health — factors that impact us and those closest to us, often with disastrous results. Branding, in fact, can be as addictive as cocaine and have just as lethal consequences.

Take, for example, the universal obsession with selfies. No risk, it seems, is too great for those who want to go "viral," hence all the images of brazen tourists going nose-to-nose with wild animals in nature preserves or safari parks, or of individuals standing close to the edge of precipices. Some years back, for example, while living in a high rise in downtown Chicago, I caught sight of a young woman straddling the guard rail on the roof deck, convulsed with laughter, while her companion snapped each death-defying pose. I made a quick phone call and, fortunately, the security guard was able to coax the duo away from danger before they landed with a splat on Jackson Boulevard. When a client shows up for coaching, it is often his or her "brand" that first walks through the door or logs onto Zoom or some other platform. It takes a skilled coach to recognize the scared child hiding behind the high-profile, risk-taking entrepreneur or to suspect that the brilliant, seemingly self-assured professor is tormented by a sense of inadequacy. Only through careful listening and observation can the coach begin to see who is really "in the room," both literally and figuratively.

What takes even greater skill, however, is guiding the client on the journey of self-discovery — *an Epiphany journey* — that will ultimately set the client free.

SUMMARY

- Many clients would prefer to maintain the *status quo* than to face the truth about themselves and their situations.
- Coaches need to ask probing questions that puncture the client's version of events. "What if" questions can be helpful here.
- Coaches need to distinguish between clients' *personas* and their real selves.
- The coaching journey is an opportunity for clients to step away from their public *personas* and embark on a journey of self-discovery.

"Fragile"

I am like an egg
Without a shell—
Soft, easily bruised,
Sensitive to the touch.
The membrane
Buffering me
From the outside world
Wears thin,
Springs back less readily
Than in days when
I could hold my own,
Fight back tears,
Control modulations
In my voice.

***

I was Spartan-born,
Trained by Stoics,
Formed by the British School
Of stiff upper lip
And all that,
But my invincible self
Has shattered
And, like the proverbial Humpty,
I am stripped
Of epidermal comfort.

Woman Dreamer, 1989

CHAPTER FOUR

Truth Is a Kaleidoscope

Encountering Multiple Truths

Behind every coaching agenda, there is a narrative — or to be more precise, there are multiple narratives. The issue is that most clients see things only from their own perspective, just as in the much-quoted parable of *The Blind Men and the Elephant*. Originating in ancient India, this parable describes how a group of blind men encounter an elephant for the first time. Relying only on touch to comprehend what the creature looks like, each man shares what he has experienced. For one, an elephant is an enormous piece of leather (the hide); for another, it is a sharp curved sword (a tusk); for another, it's a heavy, flexible pipe (the trunk); for yet another, it is a thin rope (the tail); and for another, it is a flapping fan (an ear). Clinging to their own definition of "elephant," the men cannot comprehend why everybody else in their group is lying and they come to blows. The possibility that the elephant could be the sum total of what they have experienced doesn't occur to them; instead, each assumes that the elephant is nothing more than what he has felt and touched. Precisely because they are closed to other perspectives, they will never comprehend the truth — or experience enlightenment!

Or take a group of witnesses who must provide a detailed account of the same incident. Recently, for example, I was heading to a store to purchase a winter jacket when I noticed a large crowd in front of the entrance. Handbags and small purses were scattered on the ground in front of the store in what looked like a pool of blood. Several people were supporting an elderly gentleman who was standing close by, clearly in a state of shock, blood pouring down his face. Since the injured man was being tended to and since the entrance to the store was blocked, I turned away. I saw nothing more and nothing less than what I have just described.

A bystander, however, would most likely provide a more detailed account. While I noted **a crowd + scattered merchandise + blood + an injured elderly gentleman**, the bystander might add that the same elderly gentleman lost his balance, grabbed a rack of handbags outside the store, and then fell, bringing the merchandise on top of him as he hit the ground, face first. The bystander's account would read like this: **elderly gentleman lost his balance + grabbed rack of handbags + fell + brought merchandise on top of him + hit his face + bled copiously.** Someone else, however, may have witnessed additional details. Interrogated by the police, that person might have this to say: **a pickpocket grabbed an elderly gentleman's wallet + elderly gentleman turned around to stop him + pickpocket shoved the elderly gentleman + elderly gentleman lost his balance + grabbed a rack of handbags + fell + brought merchandise on top of him + hit his face + bled copiously.**

Each narrative depends upon where the witness was at the time of the gentleman's fall and what each witness observed; each narrative is true, but the "whole truth" of the incident depends upon details others contributed as well. It may be that some members of the crowd had observed the pickpocket in action before, or that the shopkeeper had just warned the pickpocket to stop loitering on the premises, or that the elderly gentleman's wallet was in his back pocket, making him an easy target. Or it could be that the pickpocket had an accomplice, or that the two of them got away on scooters, or that someone in the crowd chased after them while others called the police and an ambulance.... When we promise to "tell the truth, the whole truth, and nothing but the truth," we can only testify to what we have seen and heard without embellishments or omissions. In fact, it can be quite a shock — *a negative Epiphany* — to discover that one's "whole truth" is limited.

One analogy I have used in classroom settings to explore the value of multiple perspectives is the definition of what a poem means. Take an esoteric poem like T. S. Eliot's *The Wasteland*. In the first place, there is the meaning that the poet intended — unless, of course, the content simply channeled through him, as poetry sometimes does, without any conscious intention on Eliot's part. Then there are all the commentaries designed to help readers understand the myriad scriptural, political, and literary references, along with the snippets of Italian, French and German. And then there is every interpretation that readers everywhere can come up with. *The Wasteland*, in fact, is constantly morphing into all the above; there is no "fixed meaning" because what it means is infinite.

So, too, with reality: it is multi-faceted and defies a one-dimensional interpretation. Along comes the client, however, with his or her story tucked between the rigid covers of a locked journal. This is the client's "truth," neatly packaged for our consumption, and, as I pointed out in the previous chapter, clients are generally reluctant to shift their mindset.

Narrative Rewards

Why are we — and our clients — so attached to our stories? In the first place, some "reward" is embedded in each narrative, whether it be gaining admiration, sympathy, fame, or simply being noticed. Whatever the reward happens to be, it feeds some dimension of our ego needs — and it takes self-reflection to recognize this. When working with clients, we need to know what drives *our* stories, if our clients are to understand the compulsions driving theirs. We cannot coach effectively unless we do our own inner work.

We can see "rewards" at work on social media where certain "friends" constantly post similar material — videos of daring exploits designed to leave lesser mortals in a state of awe, or reels of adorable children through whom the parent (or grandparent) can live vicariously, or glamor shots which elicit comments of "How good you look!" even if the subject has aged beyond recognition, or else has overdone Botox treatments. Stories, like social media posts, make us feel better about ourselves; they validate our choices, justify our failings, excuse our omissions, and generally present the version of who we believe ourselves to be. The formula goes something like this: *I am the protagonist of my story, and my story proves how unique I am!*

Now, some individuals relish being the scum of the earth, but most storytellers prefer to appear as the best versions of themselves and to camouflage the less savory details. The stories we usually tell about ourselves and about others consist of partial truths with carefully crafted embellishments; over time, we can no longer distinguish between what is true and the various fabrications. As a child, for example, I had an active imagination and developed a habit of telling tall tales for my own entertainment and to make others laugh; never once, however, did I write an essay claiming that my mother was six feet tall, drank whisky, and smoked cigars. That story was my father's creation. Whenever he shared this story at family gatherings, I would vehemently protest my innocence, but he would always insist, to my embarrassment, that, yes, Elizabeth was the author of this outrageous tale. In his mind, what he was saying was absolutely true — and the more his audience laughed, the more he believed his narrative.

Faulty Recall

Faulty recall is something else to consider when a client begins to narrate "the truth, the whole truth, and nothing but the truth." How often have witnesses testified in court that they clearly saw the defendant commit some crime when, in fact, the real perpetrator looked completely different? It is not that witnesses intend to lie, but deep-seated prejudices and assumptions can cause people to *imagine* that they have seen what they have not seen, especially when identifying the race, ethnicity, or religion of a suspect.

To complicate matters, there is the "group narrative syndrome," that is, a false story that members of a group uphold as true. Take, for example, the narrative that took on a life of its own after a fatal motorcycle accident. Witnesses swore that the motorcyclist was traveling at about 200 mph in a residential area when his bike, a Kawasaki Ninja 250R, could only reach a top speed of 105 mph. Moreover, their claim that he was texting while riding was later disproved as his mobile was safely stored in a saddlebag.

Or take the group narrative that the previous owners of my new townhouse used to dry homemade rice noodles on the frame of our community gazebo. Having purchased my home from a Chinese couple, I soon heard a collection of prejudicial stories about the previous owners. Yes, I believed that multiple generations lived in the same small space, and yes, they might have been fined by the HOA for hanging their laundry on the deck — *but rice noodles?* That is where I had to question the veracity of the communal memory.

I, myself, was once at the center of a faulty narrative, and so I am fully aware that a large group of people can believe the same erroneous account of events — in this case, that I had killed my neighbor's cat. Living in an Irish Catholic community, I not only stood out for being Anglo-Maltese but also for pulling my children out of neighborhood schools to bus them to an integrated gifted program in an African American neighborhood. In addition, I was the only mother on the block who had multiple professional commitments and who therefore didn't have much time to socialize with other parents. These factors alone made me the perfect scapegoat, especially as I had already complained that the same cat that eventually went missing had the unfortunate habit of killing birds in my backyard.

The narrative went like this: the offending cat vanished on the Fourth of July, and since I happened to leave the country to visit my family in Europe on the same day as the cat's disappearance, I must have killed the cat, hidden its corpse in my suitcase, and left the scene of the crime. Evidently, nobody considered the fact that the Fourth of July celebrations spook out everyone's pets on account of all the fireworks — legal and otherwise! I returned from my travels to discover that neighbors no longer talked to me, that my babysitter was no longer available, and that someone had "keyed" my car, leaving deep gouges on both sides.

Core Stories versus Embellished Stories

Stories take on a life of their own, accumulating details with each telling. If, as coaches, we listen to a story that has been told and retold multiple times, then we must distinguish between the "core" story and the embellished story. What are the basic facts? What seems extraneous or purely subjective? What elements of the story are suspect? What parts of the story stretch our belief? At what points in the story does the storyteller seem to have the most energy? Or the least energy? These are just some of the questions that demand our attention, even as we listen with "positive regard" towards the teller.

All this being said, when we receive a client's story, we would do well to "suspend disbelief" while maintaining a certain degree of skepticism. The term "willing suspension of disbelief" was coined by the English poet/ literary critic, Samuel Taylor Coleridge (1772–1834) to explain how readers must be willing to embrace a fictional world, no matter how implausible that world happens to be. The task of a seasoned writer, then, is to provide a "semblance of truth" so that poetic faith is possible. In coaching, these two seemingly contradictory responses — "suspension of disbelief" and skepticism — *can* co-exist. We suspend disbelief when we allow ourselves to enter our clients' worlds and see reality through their eyes, experiencing their rage, pain, elation, and triumph. We survey scene by scene, actively following each chapter while observing the storyteller's facial expressions, body language, and tone of voice. We listen intently, exuding genuine empathy and care; we make subtle vocalizations to indicate our attentive presence. When the story reaches its conclusion, we pause respectfully before speaking. Choosing our words carefully, we say something like, "I'm sorry this happened to you," or "This must have been a major setback!" or "I'm so happy you were able to turn this situation around!" or simply, "Thank you for sharing!"

Then comes the challenge. What parts of the story seem embellished? Where do the narrator's assumptions and biases seem apparent? What other perspectives are needed to flesh out this narrative's reality and separate fact from fiction? As coaches, we have only milliseconds to sort out our reactions and make sense of what we have heard — unless, of course, we return to the narrative later in the session or during another meeting. As a fan of the PBS series, *All Creatures Great and Small*, I have been intrigued by the relationship between the short-tempered, authoritarian Siegfried Farnon, a middle-aged veterinarian in pre-World War II rural England, and his impulsive, irresponsible younger brother, Tristan. From Siegfried's point of view, Tristan is a party-loving spendthrift who often fails to follow instructions and then lies about it; from Tristan's perspective, Siegfried is a stern father figure with unrealistic expectations. The truth finally comes out in the final episode of Season Three. In a powerful, tear-jerker of a scene, we learn that Siegfried was always jealous of Tristan because their parents favored their youngest son the most; moreover, he resented having to be responsible for Tristan and for having to be a father figure to him. For his part, Tristan wanted nothing more than to win his brother's approval but felt like a complete failure. Only when they shared their narratives could the brothers create a new narrative based on genuine affection and mutual respect. The "Truth" of Siegfried and Tristan's relationship, then, involved more than one story; their *Epiphany* was to know that despite their differences and mutually antagonistic behaviors, they genuinely loved each other.

SUMMARY

- Behind every coaching agenda, there are multiple narratives.
- Most clients tend to see things only from their perspective.
- We become attached to our narratives because there is usually some reward embedded in each story.
- Stories tend to consist of partial truths and carefully crafted embellishments.
- Group narratives are often influenced by faulty recall and/or underlying bias.
- Coaches need to receive clients' stories both with "suspension of disbelief" and healthy skepticism.
- Truth involves multiple perspectives.

"Witch Hunt"

She said
I killed her cat—
Poisoned it, no doubt,
Flayed it alive
Before flinging
The cadaver
In the garbage can.
When she looked,
There was nothing there—
Not one feline hair
Of accusation.
She said
I did it
All the same,
Now waits
To find its tail
Nailed to her door
While I,
Securely tied,
Burn before trial.

Frost and Fire, 1985

CHAPTER FIVE

Deciphering the Subtext

Coaching versus Therapy

As coaches, we know that one of the cardinal sins is to cross the line into practicing therapy with a coaching client. Such a transgression, in fact, violates the *International Coaching Federation's Code of Ethics*, putting us at risk of disciplinary action and even of the loss of our coveted coaching credential. While therapists dive into the murky past, helping patients identify demons in the unconscious that distort their thoughts, feelings, and behaviors, life coaches and their clients focus on what is happening in the present through a collaborative process that leads to the best possible future outcomes. Another way of looking at this is to say that therapists slay dragons and delve into cesspits while coaches open cage doors so their clients can cross bridges, climb mountains, and overcome limitations. The problem here is that the key to the cage may lie at the bottom of the cesspit, and, on some occasions, the only way upward and forward is to glance backwards.

From the outset of a coaching relationship, both coach and client typically know the difference between therapy and coaching, and, typically again, the coaching *"Welcome Package"* contains a statement reflecting this. My *Welcome Package*, for example, asks the client to agree to the following clauses:

- I am fully responsible for my well-being during the coaching agreement, including choices and decisions that may emerge from Life Coaching.
- I am aware that Life Coaching is not a substitute for psychotherapy; nor does it treat mental disorders as defined by the American Psychiatric Association.

- I promise that if I am under the care of a mental health professional, I will consult my therapist regarding the advisability of working with a life coach and let my life coach know that I am working with another professional.
- I understand that Life Coaching is not to be used as a substitute for professional advice regarding financial, medical, legal, and business issues or any other issues.

Hidden Agendas

With this kind of clarity, then, how might the coach-client relationship run into difficulty? One answer is that in addition to the stated, coaching-appropriate agenda, hidden agendas may lurk beneath the surface. Of course, neither the coach nor the client is aware that this is the case but at some point during their working together, the "subtext" might manifest just as in a play or film there are those "lines between the lines" and "hidden meanings." But while writers intentionally add subtexts to their work to build suspense, complexity and intrigue, subtexts in life coaching and other guided conversations generally emerge from the unconscious, often without warning.

Let's imagine that a client has signed up for career coaching. During the initial coaching conversation, we learn that he has taught at primary school level for about ten years, earning recognition for turning around the most challenging students. He loves his work but wants to change careers, as "it's time for something new." The conversation goes something like this:

COACH: "So, what do you love the most about teaching?"
CLIENT: "There's something awesome about seeing the light go on for kids, to see them suddenly begin to think critically and use their imaginations. There's real power in that!"
COACH: "What else?"
CLIENT: "Well, I think teaching is in my genes — both my parents were elementary school teachers, and one of my

grandparents was a college professor. I always knew I was meant to teach!"

COACH: "It sounds as though you find teaching very rewarding—"

CLIENT: "Yes, but the pay isn't that great."

COACH: "But it was for ten years?"

CLIENT: "I suppose so — I mean, I never really gave it much thought."

COACH: "So why has salary become important to you now?"

CLIENT: "I've just returned from my 15-year high school reunion — I was the only primary school teacher in the group."

COACH: "And?"

CLIENT: "Everyone else was successful — stockbrokers, lawyers, brain surgeons... They all amounted to something."

COACH: "What I'm hearing you say is that you don't feel successful when you compare yourself to your classmates and that being a teacher makes you feel inferior."

CLIENT: "Precisely. It's like we're on different playing fields — they're the players, and I'm just the ball boy."

COACH: "What is a player?"

CLIENT: "Someone who is in the game, calls the shots, wins the trophy."

COACH: "And a ball boy?"

CLIENT: "The kid left out of the game, the runt, the non-player, the loser."

As you can see, the topic of career change has morphed into a conversation around the client's sense of inadequacy. While the presenting issue was, "It's time for a career change," the real issue — the subtext — is the client's deep-seated conviction that he is a failure. This is the *"Eureka!"* moment for both coach and client, but it most likely spells the end of the coaching relationship. Ethically speaking, the coach should not assist the client in exploring new career paths when the client's agenda is driven by his negative self-image, not by a *real* desire to change professions. With a skilled therapist, however, the client can return to his high school days or earlier and re-visit what it felt like to be the "runt" of the class and how this feeling has impacted his personal and professional life. Then, he will be ready for coaching.

Touchstone Moments

This is not to say that visiting the past is an absolute taboo in coaching; at times, going back in time can yield the missing key or *Epiphany* to which I alluded earlier. Let's return to the same coach and client. The conversation has reached the point where the client has explained why he loves teaching so much:

> **COACH:** "Can you recall a moment where you felt most fulfilled as a teacher?"
>
> **CLIENT:** "There have been many such moments, but the one that stands out is when I put my class of third graders into small groups, and each group had to create a skit about what it was like to be bullied. One group focused on being fat-shamed, another on what it was like to be bullied because of religious differences, yet another portrayed someone who was treated badly on account of race, another on being bullied because the kid was an immigrant — and so on. The skits were amazing, and after that, class dynamics completely changed — everyone was a little nicer. You could literally feel it!"
>
> **COACH:** "I can feel it listening to you! Thinking ahead, what kind of work opportunities might allow you to get in touch with similar feelings?"
>
> **CLIENT:** "Well..."

In this version of the conversation, briefly going back in time allows a "touchstone moment" to surface, a moment that holds the key to what the client *really* wants to do. Here, it is neither salary that motivates him, nor the need to prove himself; instead, he connects with his desire to bring about change, to shift prejudices, to help children understand what it is to be like to be on the receiving end of bullying. With his coach's help, he is now in a better position to explore careers that will gratify him in the same way and possibly allow him to have a greater impact on shifting consciousness. His sense of wanting something "new" may not equate to leaving behind the world of teaching but may point to his need for a wider audience —possibly at the school district or even the state level.

Subtexts

I should point out that it is not just a different question that has led to this *Epiphany Moment*. Rather, in the first case, the client's deep-seated emotional issues drove his desire for a career change; in the second, his commitment to making a difference in children's lives is the driving force. Regardless of the coach's questions, a subtext will reveal itself one way or another — the coach doesn't create it!

Subtexts appear in daily life, and the more we learn to recognize them, the more we will be able to hear what our clients are really saying. A friend — or one's partner —might complain, "You are always SO busy!" What he or she might be saying is, "I miss you — can't you make time for me?" Or a colleague may joke about your absenteeism at work; the subtext could be, "I have to carry your workload when you're MIA!" Someone else may criticize you for spending too much on something they deem a luxury; the subtext here might be, "I don't have any discretionary income, so why should you?"

When a subtext surfaces, the coach needs to assess what this means for the coaching relationship. Can this subtext be included in the original coaching agreement, or will coach and client need to renegotiate the contract? For example, a team leader has signed up for coaching to explore how she might be more effective in her role; meanwhile, the emerging subtext reveals that the main issue is that her direct reports are sexist and do not respect her. This subtext adds a new twist to the original coaching agreement but by no means sabotages it. Having identified the problem, coach and client can now explore what effective leadership might look like, given the team's makeup. In fact, the subtext will allow the sessions to go deeper and lead to more satisfying results.

In contrast, if that same team leader were to discover that she has a hard time trusting any men on the team because of issues dating back to childhood, then this might be a time to recommend therapy in addition to coaching or else to pause coaching altogether while the client works on her healing. Either way, the subtext has served its purpose and leads the client towards greater integration and self-knowledge.

SUMMARY

- Coaching focuses forwards while emotional issues from the past typically need to be addressed in therapy.
- In coaching, subtexts often emerge from the unconscious without warning, surprising both coach and client.
- Sometimes, healthy "touchstone moments" manifest when visiting the past in a non-therapeutic way.
- Subtexts often surface in daily life when someone's comments hide a deeper meaning; they can lead clients to greater self-awareness.

"Roots"

Sometimes,
We do not know
They are there.
Perhaps we do not see,
Feel, or even remember
That beneath the tangling
Live-dead branches,
The congeries of leaves,
The twisted trunk,
Are roots—
Tender, succulent,
Easily bruised.

***

And in these roots
Is Mystery—
Awesome
God-given
Undeniable
Undefiable
Below ground
Yet very much alive.

***

Roots
Are not to be tampered with
For when you strip bark
Cut twigs
Gash trunk

***

Only they remain…

***

Frost and Fire, 1985

CHAPTER SIX

Crossing Over into the Client's Experience

Defining "Crossing Over"

Whenever a new client walks through the door — whether literally or figuratively — the challenge is to move beyond what we "know" so we are better equipped to understand the client's worldview. This does not mean abandoning our perspective or core values — far from it — but it does involve stretching, sometimes beyond our comfort levels. Without "crossing over" into the client's world, we cannot listen deeply enough to comprehend what is being said or left unsaid; nor can we experience that empathy which is so critical for the client's growth in self-awareness.

As we listen to another's story, we need to understand its underlying drivers and unspoken motivations. If we cling to our worldview, we will hear and respond to the surface meaning but miss the deeper meanings. Seeing through our lenses, we may completely miss the real issues at play. This, of course, will limit our ability to ask the right questions or help guide our clients toward an action plan. Worse still, our clients will leave feeling unheard and unappreciated.

Underlying Drivers and Unspoken Motivations

"Crossing over" is an essential skill in any human interaction, not just in coaching or other forms of inner guidance. For example, a child's tantrum is simply a tantrum unless the adult in charge takes the time to understand what has triggered the outburst. Too often, a child's "acting out" makes the adult frustrated, angry, or even punitive. Instead of exploring the "why" of the situation, the adult reacts, determined to maintain control through any means, whether through coercion, a raised voice, threats, or various forms of punishment.

I remember an incident from my childhood that could have played out very differently. I was about 2 or 3 years of age, and my older sister was at school. Left to my own devices, I was bored and lonely, with no other children to interact with and not an adult in sight. My attention focused on Diana's carousel, a beautifully hand-carved music box with an assortment of colorful circus animals that rotated as the music played. Unfortunately, I didn't know how to turn on the music, and despite all my efforts, the animals remained motionless. *The solution?* To break off the lions, tigers, horses, camels, and elephants, one by one, thereby liberating them from their frozen state.

The menagerie and I enjoyed each other's company until my sister came home; then, there were wails, shouts, and a spanking. Nobody ever asked why I had broken the carousel; nor did anyone consider that this was not a malicious act. In my mind, I had helped the animals by giving them the freedom to roam and participate in the stories I was creating. To my surprise, they couldn't return to the carousel, even when I tried to reconnect them to their wooden home. The possibility that I had broken my sister's much-beloved treasure never crossed my mind.

"There but for the Grace of God..."

One of my dad's favorite sayings used to be *"There but for the grace of God..."* This saying typically surfaced when we were out as a family — either riding in the car to attend Sunday Mass or else when we were seated at a restaurant. One of us — and we were four sisters — upon noticing someone behaving erratically or dressed strangely, would pass a loud comment so the rest of the family could hear. That was when Dad would interject,

"There but for the grace of God..." What he was asking us to do was not only be aware of the blessings we enjoyed but to "cross over" into what life was like for the person who had disrupted our carefree thoughts.

I remember taking this quite seriously at times. Once, for example, when I was about 5 or 6 years old, we were seated at an outdoor café in the *Piazza San Marco* in Venice when a ragged beggar approached our table with outstretched hands and a toothless smile. Assuming she needed sugar, I emptied the bowl of sugar lumps into her weathered hands. Looking at me in astonishment, she pocketed the sugar and shuffled towards an adjacent table. Pleased to have helped her out, I didn't understand why the adults seemed to think there was something amusing about my actions. After all, there but for the grace of God, I might have been without sugar lumps for my freshly squeezed lemon juice...

Becoming the Buddha

Recognizing that the suffering we observe in others could have been our lot and could be what we ourselves might endure in the future is a powerful spiritual exercise. In fact, beholding suffering for the first time led Prince Siddhartha Gautama to embark on his spiritual journey. According to legend, his father had sheltered him from anything unpleasant to keep him on track to becoming a powerful ruler. A prophecy at Siddhartha's birth predicted that he would either be a mighty king or a great spiritual leader, but the prince's father was determined that his son would inherit the throne. Therefore, he created an environment where the prince would experience nothing but privilege and delight.

Having been raised with every luxury and distraction, from bevies of dancing girls to the choicest sherbet, the prince ventured from his palace in his chariot one day. Unbeknownst to his son, the king had issued a royal decree banning any signs of poverty, illness, or decay from the streets. Despite this decree, Siddhartha noted four disturbing sights on this and three other outings. In response to his question, *"What is that?"* the charioteer replied:

"That is **old age**, my Lord, the fate of every human being!"

"That is **sickness,** my Lord, the fate of every human being!"

"That is **death,** my Lord, the fate of every human being!"

"That is **meditation,** my Lord, the invitation to every human being to master suffering!"

And thus it was that through those harsh *Epiphanies* the Buddha — the enlightened one — was born.

Only by being able to "cross over" into the shoes of others can we understand what they are going through. Just as Siddhartha saw old age, sickness, and death for the first time, so we need to understand what these realities mean to those around us, as well as to our clients. What would it be like if we experienced life from their perspective, wearing their shoes? Or what would it be like to lose our job, to be passed over for promotion, to be disgraced publicly, to experience racism or sexism in the workplace, to be undermined by a colleague, to be falsely accused, to lose a loved one, to have no security? *How would we feel? How would our circumstances change? How would we cope? Who would stand by us? What resources would we lack?*

Cultural Drivers and Motivations

Sometimes, drivers and motivations are cultural and originate in worlds very different from ours. Take, for example, the problems brought to relationship coaching by an inter-cultural couple. The male is Indian, from India; his partner was born and raised in the United States but is of Italian descent. They are planning on getting married but have run into communication difficulties. When the Bride-to-be says "wedding," she pictures a traditional ceremony in a Catholic church — the white dress, an entourage of bridesmaids, walking down the aisle on her father's arm, a full-length mass, a soloist singing *Ave Maria*...

For his part, the Groom-to-be imagines a celebration spanning several days, involving multiple rituals, hundreds of guests, elaborate attire for each day, and endless feasting.

On the surface, it might seem that a conversation around "compromise" is the logical solution; however, more is going on that needs to be addressed. For the Bride-to-be, a secular wedding is not an option. Without a "Church blessing," her marriage would be considered invalid. Moreover, she not only has to receive a dispensation from the diocesan bishop but must also promise to continue practicing the faith and to raise any children as Catholic. Then, of course, are the expectations of her family. Already, many of her relatives are shocked that she is engaged to someone they consider "pagan," and she knows that most of them will refuse to attend the Indian nuptials. As for the Groom-to-be, many of his relatives will be traveling from India for the wedding and he also belongs to a sizable Indian community in the States. Like his fiancée's family, his relatives have religious and cultural expectations, and he would be dishonoring both his parents and his community should he try to simplify the nuptials. A further complication is that the groom's family usually pays for the wedding in Italy, whereas in India, it is the bride's family. Though the Hindu wedding is by far going to be the costlier of the ceremonies and though the Bride-to-be's family is likely to be absent, yet the cultural expectation is that her parents should cover the cost. Conversely, the "pagan" Hindus — *and, of course, I am using the word in a derogatory sense to reflect how the Bride-to-be's family feels* — have an obligation to pay for the Christian ceremony.

When the couple meets with their coach for the first time, they share their differing expectations for their wedding and express the *impasse* they have reached in their planning. If their coach has listened only at a surface level, then the response will be to focus on compromise and problem-solving. If, however, the coach — who may not share any of the couple's cultural communities — can "cross over" into their respective worlds, then he or she is more likely to help these clients make the same journey. Once the Bride-to-be and the Groom-to-be understand all that's at stake religiously, culturally, and financially, they may see new options. No longer frustrated with each other, they now see through different lenses and can stand together as they face the seemingly insurmountable difficulties presented by their approaching marriage.

Learning How to "Cross Over"

"Crossing over" takes practice and flexibility. As an English teacher, I often created assignments designed to teach my college students what it is like to be the "differing other." For example, dividing the students in my English 101 College Writing classes into pairs, I created the following rubric for their *Ethnographic Essay/Collaborative Writing Project*:

Topic: Your task is to select a group, with a study partner, to which you do NOT belong and to present this group as faithfully as you can to your classmates so that they, too, may "cross over" into a new experience of "the differing other." The writing skills required include summary, narration, description, explanation, interviewing skills and personal reflection.

1. Please select a "safe" group (no gang infiltration, please!) that you can access freely on or off campus, according to your schedule. Ideally, find a group about which you have little prior knowledge.
2. Begin with your assumptions/ biases about this group, followed by some preliminary research (review websites, Wikipedia, promotional materials, newspaper files). I'm not asking you to write a research paper or to use scholarly sources. You can

> *Google your group to give you an overview of what it stands for, (for example, its core beliefs, membership base, activities, contributions to society, etc.).*
> 3. *Attend some of the group's activities — a protest march, a meeting, a performance, a religious service, a presentation — making sure to chronicle your observations and experiences.*
> 4. *Interview at least 2 leaders or members of this group and incorporate their comments into your paper.*
> 5. *You and your study partner will each hand in a separate assignment. Only 2 students may work on the same group/same topic.*

*Please note that you must document all your encounters with this group and that merely interviewing a roommate will not earn you a passing grade. Make sure you select your group carefully, leaving enough time in the semester to connect in a meaningful way. Please do not endanger yourself by getting involved with cults, gangs, or the criminal underground; also, make sure you do your homework **before** contacting the group.*

As you can see, the rubric involved various skills and activities, starting with fieldwork. Having selected their respective groups, the students had to acquire as much firsthand experience as possible. Before attending events or interviewing group members, they researched their groups online, visiting websites and social media sites, examining mission statements, and browsing through reviews, press releases, public records, and personal testimonials. After that, they were responsible for contacting their group to explain the project and find out when they might visit. If the group were open to hosting them, then the students' next task was to clarify whom they could interview, what they should wear, and if there were any "rules" they needed to observe — for example, covering up tattoos, not shaking hands, removing shoes inside a sacred space, turning off mobiles. Before the actual visit, each pair was to draw up a list of questions they could make available to their hosts prior to the interviews, should this be requested. They also took down the group leaders' names, titles, and contact information.

Just as my students prepared themselves to enter new worlds, coaches will be better equipped to work with clients from other cultures if they do their homework. Clients do not leave their language, race, ethnicity, religion, gender, sexual preferences, beliefs, traditions, socio-economic class, educational background, political affiliations, and other variables outside our office doors — or off Zoom calls. Rather, they show up in all their uniqueness, hoping to find empathy and understanding. This is where first encounters and *The Welcome Package* come in.

When we meet with a prospective coaching client to explore if there is a good professional fit, we have an opportunity to identify some of the "differences" that surface in that conversation — and make note of them! Then, should we move to the onboarding stage, we can provide a *Welcome Package* that not only asks specific questions but also invites our new client to share a brief autobiography. Again, we take notes, do some research, and ensure we understand the various "communities" to which our client belongs.

Going back to the intercultural couple, imagine that you, the coach, know nothing about Hinduism or Catholicism, nor about Indian and Italian wedding traditions and cultural norms. If the couple were to decide to retain your services as coach, it would be advisable to do your "homework" before the first official session. This could mean surfing the net for such basics as "Catholic beliefs about marriage," "Catholic beliefs about intermarriage with non-Christians," "Catholic wedding traditions," "Hindu beliefs about marriage," "Hindu beliefs about intermarriage with non-Hindus," and "Hindu wedding traditions." Such research would not only provide details about differing wedding celebrations but also explain why the families of both bride and groom are likely to be unhappy with the match. For example, for Catholics a marriage is only considered "sacramental" if both parties are baptized; similarly, for most Hindus, a marriage would be considered valid only if both partners are Hindu.

Such research can take as little as 15–30 minutes, but it provides the coach with invaluable cultural frameworks from which "the right questions" can surface. Unless the coach has a basic understanding of the conflicting world views that have shaped these clients, there is not much chance of anyone moving beyond current thinking, let alone reaching that much longed-for "Ah-ha" moment.

SUMMARY

- "Crossing over" into the client's experience facilitates listening, understanding, and empathy.
- To listen deeply, coaches need to be aware of underlying drivers and unspoken motivations.
- Working effectively with clients from "communities" other than our own requires "homework."
- *The Welcome Package* offers the opportunity to learn more about a client before the first coaching session.

no

"Cosmic Wheel"

I see a wheel
Luminous shafts converging
At the still hub
Of the turning circle
Where unitive fire
Fuses differences
Into explosive energy
Burning
Without consuming
Blazing
Without blinding
Illuminating the darkness
In a chain reaction
Of glowing intensity.

***

I desire
That voracious fire
That conflagration of love;
I hunger for those sparks
Of fervent flame
Which burnish
Add luster
Give sheen
To what is commonplace
And dull.

***

As the wheel spins
And spokes turn

The fire spreads
From hub to perimeter
Kindling a multitude
Of paths
With its searing truth
And passionate light.

***

And each way
Is good...

***

Woman Dreamer, 1989

CHAPTER SEVEN

Unknowing and Exploring the Unknown

The Coaching Engagement

When clients sign up for coaching, they typically seek new knowledge or awareness, whether this be about overcoming bad habits, developing better communication skills, improving relationships, building a business, preparing for a career change, or handling difficult employees. Regardless of the presenting issue or issues, coach and client embark on a journey of discovery with specific goals in mind. During the coaching conversation, they collaborate on developing a plan of action, along with methods of accountability. Simply put, there is a starting point which we could name *"Where Things Are Now"* and an ending spot we could call *"Where We Want to Be"*; in the middle lies *"Unknown Territory."* This place of "unknowing" holds the key to the coaching outcomes.

Let's look at a simple scenario. A client hires a life coach to improve her work-life balance. She is fully aware that something needs to change as she is putting in 70-hour work weeks as a corporate attorney while raising a teenage son, caring for her mother who has dementia, handling her deceased father's estate, and serving on the board of the local community college. When asked why work-life balance is important to her, the client shares a list of "red flags" — high blood pressure, weight gain, headaches, exhaustion, social anxiety, depression, irritability, brain fog, resentment towards her mother, and an inability to relate to her son who is flunking most of his high school courses. Her desired outcome, not surprisingly, is to have a happier, healthier life. Since the client is well-aware of *Where Things Are Now* and what she hopes to gain from the coaching engagement, it is the *Unknown Territory* that will be the focus.

With the client's list of "red flags," the coach might be tempted to address issue by issue — perhaps one or two per session — identifying action plans for each. It would be all too easy to say, *"High blood pressure?* What healthy habits might lower the numbers?" Or *"Exhaustion?* How much sleep are you getting?" Or, again, *"Your son?* What do his guidance counselors have to say?"

This approach, however, addresses the symptoms rather than core problems and skims across the *Unknown Territory* while providing quick fixes that the client could have come up with herself. In effect, the coach would be focusing on the parts rather than the whole, rather like an entourage of doctors who each examine a patient from the vantage point of their specialties without ever consulting each other. Now, it is true that the exhausted client is looking for solutions, but *Unknown Territory* holds the keys that can bring about a mind shift and create a brand-new way of living.

When the coach settles for problem-solving instead of exploration, the client misses out on life-changing discoveries. Addressing the "red flags" one by one might provide some temporary relief for the client but is unlikely to yield lasting results. True, it may help the client move beyond *Where Things Are Now* to *Where We Want to Be,* but it completely ignores the rich territory of the *Unknown.*

Unknown Territory

A skilled coach is not afraid to linger in *Unknown Territory,* even if doing so delays achieving the client's desired outcomes. What might intrigue the coach is the possibility that the "red flags" collectively point to an unnamed underlying issue. Instead of addressing the symptoms — that is, the headaches, weight gain, irritability, etc. — the coach instead leads the client on some sort of *Wheel of Life* analysis. The results might read something like this:

Personal Relationships: Client tries hard, cannot set boundaries or limits, becomes frustrated and resentful.

World of Work: Client is carrying more than her fair share of the workload, brings work home, cannot keep up, becomes exhausted.

Civic Responsibilities: Client is active on the board of the local community college but at the expense of leisure time/ personal time.

Having established the context of the client's symptoms, the coach might now ask some additional questions:

COACH: "So, as you look at your personal relationships, the world of work, and civic responsibilities, what do they share in common?"
CLIENT: "Well, they're all contributing to my burnout."
COACH: "Agreed, but what is driving you to invest so much of yourself in each area?"
CLIENT: "Someone has to do it. If I don't pick up the slack when my colleagues go home, we will fall behind with drafting court docs and checking briefs. And if I don't take care of my mother, none of my siblings will — she's living with me right now and has got to the stage when she cannot be left alone. As for my son, I'm the one with custody — his father is not involved."
COACH: "And the community college?"
CLIENT: "They needed someone with a legal background on the board and wanted female representation — it was by invitation."
COACH: "'Someone has to do it.' It seems you are carrying the burdens others don't want."
CLIENT: "That's the story of my life."

COACH: "Can you say more about that?"

CLIENT: "I've always had to take charge. I basically raised my kid brothers as my mom was an alcoholic and my dad wasn't around. As early as pre-school, I was ahead of my classmates, so the teachers made me help them with their homework, so I wouldn't be bored — this continued through grad school, if you can believe it..."

COACH: "So how might you re-write this story?"

Unknown Territory has yielded the client's life-long pattern of assuming responsibility when others fail to "show up" or do their work well. She has lived by the *False-Self Narrative*, "If I don't do it, nobody will." This, in turn, has affected every aspect of her life, from professional commitments to personal obligations, and the price she has paid is sacrificing her own physical, emotional, and spiritual well-being. This life-changing revelation can now guide future coaching conversations around "next steps." Possible actions include meeting with her colleagues to discuss an equitable distribution of work; coming up with a plan of action for her mother's care that includes her siblings; resigning from the board of the local community college; spending more time with her son and enjoying shared interests together; and designing a "health recovery" program to lessen and eventually eliminate the physical problems that have surfaced in her life.

Each of these actions, however, may require a different strategy that could also become a coaching focus. For example, the conversation the client has with her colleagues will be different than the one she has with her siblings. In the first instance, the client may decide to share details of her workload while explaining what each person on the team could do to make the division of labor more equitable. Her approach will be factual, demonstrable, and unemotional; she will appeal to reason and invite discussion.

In her conversation with her siblings, however, the starting point might be to share their mother's rapid cognitive decline and what this means in terms of her care. The client might also provide information regarding the typical trajectory of dementia and what the future will likely hold. While focusing on the logistics of caring for their mother — for example, having to employ caregivers during work hours and scheduling medical appointments — the client might also address how exhausted she is feeling. As in the conversation with her colleagues, the client presents "the facts," but this time appeals to her siblings' empathy.

Unknown Territory, then, has not only identified an unhealthy pattern as the root of the client's lack of work-life balance but has also provided some actionable steps and helpful conversational strategies to accomplish them. Instead of merely encouraging the client to identify "band-aid" solutions, the coach has helped her acquire a sense of agency — empowerment, if you will — and to embark on a path of self-care for perhaps the first time in her life.

Identifying False-Self Narratives

The client in the previous case study seems driven by *"The Savior"* archetype or pattern of being. I will be addressing archetypes in Chapter Thirteen, but for now it is enough to say that archetypes are patterns that surface in all cultures, in all eras, and that there are distinctive characteristics for each archetype. *The Savior*, for example, is a heroic archetype that involves self-sacrifice for the sake of others. Though noble in its reach, this archetype can drive individuals to neglect their own interests, avoid delegating, and ignore obvious solutions to many of the problems they encounter; instead, those "possessed" by this archetype embrace *False-Self Narratives* like *"If I don't do it, nobody else will,"* or *"I am the only one who can fix this problem,"* or *"I can achieve better results working on my own than collaborating with others."*

A *False-Self Narrative* is an autobiographical story that we believe to be true, even though it is based on lies. Since clients are seldom aware that their worldview has been shaped by the *False-Self*, it can be difficult for the coach to see this as well — and, of course, to lead clients into self-awareness. When traversing — or excavating — *Unknown Territory* with our clients, we would do well to be on the lookout for any *False-Self Narratives* that may be hiding in plain view and to realize that more than one such narrative might be involved. For example, returning to the previous case study, there are signs that the client is also driven by *The People Pleaser Narrative*. Unable to stand up to her clients, siblings, or even her teenage son, the attorney may believe that if she expresses her frustration, asks for help, or resigns from her *"Savior"* role, everyone will hate her. Her *People Pleaser Narrative* goes something like this: *"I am only acceptable if I take care of everyone, never complain, and never set boundaries. If I let them know how I really feel, I will ruin all my relationships."* The combination of *The Savior* archetype with a *People Pleaser Narrative* has left the client ill-equipped to lead a balanced life. Multiple *False-Self Narratives* shape our consciousness, and as long as they form the dominant story, there is little hope that we will experience a mind shift of any kind. These stories trap us into repeated thoughts and actions that can detrimentally affect our work, play, relationships, health, and even futures.

False-Self Narratives fall into two main categories: those that make us imagine we are better than we really are and those that whittle away at our sense of self and worthiness. In the first category, we find stories of entitlement: *"I am better than everyone else," "I am entitled to the good things of this life," "I deserve this position," "I can get by on my looks," "The company can't function without me," "I am indispensable for this project," "Nobody else can do this as well as I can," "Everyone is jealous of my accomplishments," "I should not have to pay for my mistakes," "I am above the law," "I deserve more recognition," "Other people are lucky* to know me," "I deserve to be the center of the universe," "My brand is ME!"

In the second category, there are stories of the diminished self: *"I don't have what it takes," "I am doomed to failure," "I will never succeed in life," "I am unlovable," "I will be a failure like my dad," "I'm never going to find the right mate," "I'm the black sheep of the family," "Other people are more talented than I am," "I don't have any gifts," " I don't deserve to be happy," "I will never be able to break this cycle," "I'm unlucky," "I've nothing to say of value," "I don't have a purpose in life," "I'm simply a burden to others and have nothing to contribute," "I never have any good luck," "I lead a boring life," "Nobody is interested in what I have to say..."*

Both egotistical narratives and self-effacing narratives block us from accepting the truth about ourselves and from moving into a healthier, happier future. Sometimes, past events reinforce the false beliefs behind these stories; sometimes, other people's words or our own persistent thoughts get in the way of re-writing old scripts. As a result, the *False-Self Narratives* continue to grip us, sometimes gaining power with the passage of time.

Effective coaching, however, can provide strategies for transforming habitual, self-defeating stories into stories with more productive outcomes. The first step is for clients to notice how *False-Self Narratives* not only drive them but also limit them. For example, if clients believe that it's their task to make their team members happy, they will never hold them accountable or be able to disagree with them. The challenge is to shift non-productive, self-destructive ways of thinking to create a brand-new story.

When clients recognize the forces at play, they can choose new endings to the old scripts — if they dare imagine life-giving options! Our task is to help our clients move from *False-Self Narratives* into authentic stories that are aligned with their vision, mission, and purpose. We can also help them play with the components of story to transform memories, present experiences, and future outcomes. During a coaching session, the coach must pay attention to the client's words and images, especially to repeated utterances. A simple statement like *"I haven't taken a vacation in years"* may indicate that the client focuses on the world of work to the exclusion of personal time; similarly, the client who complains about mandatory DEIJ training (Diversity, Equity, Inclusion and Justice) may be oblivious to the challenges minorities experience daily and may lack compassion when it comes to the needs of direct reports. Or take the CEO who continually refers to his female employees as "the gals" — his choice of words indicates an outdated view of women and the inability to view them as professionals. Or take the team leader who uses "I" whenever she refers to work on current projects; in her mind, the contributions of the rest of the team are irrelevant, or she would use the first-person plural. "What's in a pronoun?" you might say. Well, if you are a team member who sees the leader take all the glory and seize all the rewards, the answer would be *"Everything."*

SUMMARY

- Coaching clients typically seek some new knowledge or awareness.
- The starting point is *Where Things Are Now* while the end spot is *Where We Want to Be*; in the middle lies *Unknown Territory*.
- Coaches need to distinguish between symptoms and core issues.
- *Unknown Territory* usually holds the key to the ***real*** issues in contrast to the stated issues.
- There are multiple *False-Self Narratives*, some of which inflate the self and others which diminish it.
- Coaches can identify *False-Self Narratives* through the client's words and images.

"Ambiguity"

I have heard
There are ways
Of knowing
What is of God
And what is not,
Of distinguishing revelation
From wild imaginings
And neurological impulses.

***

I, for one,
Recall the burning certitude
Of Presence,
The searing light
Of blessed assurance
And amazing grace.
I have unfastened sandals
And stood on holy ground,
Cradled in fire,
Absorbed in rapture.
I have known
The Cloud of Unknowing,
The embrace of the Bridegroom.

***

And yet, I am still
Plagued by uncertainties
And unresolved enigmas,
Pursued by darkness,
Hounded down

By chaos.
The hunt is on;
Frenzied dogs pant
At my heels,
Leaping after me,
Pitiless jaws
Gaping wide as death,
And whether they are heaven-sent
Or hell-bent, I will flee,
Holding them at bay.

Woman Dreamer, 1989

CHAPTER EIGHT

Rigid Mindsets

During a coaching engagement, a coach may notice that the client tends to have a *"Rigid Mindset"* regarding certain topics — or all topics, for that matter! Now, *Rigid Mindsets* are nothing new. Most of us have seen them exhibited in multiple settings and may even exhibit them ourselves. They occur when we think in terms of dichotomies — *either/or, good/bad, right/wrong,* or *black/white,* with no shades of grey or pinko-grey in between. Such thinking cannot tolerate the *Unknown Territory* described in the previous chapter; on the contrary, it wants definitive answers, rejecting the possibility that "perhaps" or "maybe" exist or that options might be worth exploring. In the coaching engagement, this effectively sabotages any discovery process or the creation of "actionable steps." There are no steps to take because the client's mindset is cast in stone.

The Poverty Mindset

One common mindset — popularly named the *"Poverty Mindset"* — is the tendency to see a glass half-empty instead of half-full. No matter how much abundance there is in a person's life, he or she will focus on what is missing. Ironically, the very wealthy are often plagued by this syndrome. Despite impressive financial portfolios and vast real estate holdings, they are paranoid about the future and feel they lack security. Enough is never enough.

Sometimes, children seem to be born with the "half-empty glass" syndrome. Take twins who each receive identical Christmas stockings; one child rips open the contents of his stocking, barely examining the various toys and treats inside until there is nothing more to unwrap and in contrast, the other child opens each item slowly, squealing with delight as she does so. The first twin is clearly disappointed and wants to know where his other presents are hiding; meanwhile, the second twin is so absorbed with her gifts that she loses all sense of time. One child sees lack, while the other sees abundance.

A *Poverty Mindset* can also be learned. Adults who grew up in a household where the constant refrain was, *"There must be more money! There must be more money!"* grow up feeling poor. D. H. Lawrence captures this syndrome in his tragic short story *The Rocking-Horse Winner* (1926). A couple with expensive tastes lived beyond their means, and the mother — a beautiful woman with no heart — was obsessed with their financial situation, even letting her children know that they were the poor members of the family and that she was the unlucky wife of an unlucky husband:

> And so the house came to be haunted by the unspoken phrase: "There must be more money! There must be more money!" The children could hear it all the time, though nobody said it aloud. They heard it at Christmas when the expensive and splendid toys filled the nursery. Behind the shining modern rocking-horse, behind the smart doll's house, a voice would start whispering: "There must be more money! There must be more money!" And the children would stop playing to listen for a moment. They would look into each other's eyes, to see if they had all heard. And each one saw in the eyes of the other two that they too had heard. "There must be more money! There must be more money."

Sadly, we never learn how this *Poverty Mindset* would affect the children in their adult years as Paul, the couple's only son, was so determined to solve the family's financial problems by bringing them luck that he died in the process. His secret was that whenever he frenziedly rode his rocking horse, the name of a winning racehorse would come to mind. Aided and abetted by his uncle and the gardener, he amassed a small fortune at the Ascot races whilst also making them rich.

His uncle ensured that Paul's mother received his nephew's winnings without letting her know the source of this income, but nothing seemed to satisfy her. Finally, Paul rode his last race, rocking madly on his toy horse until the winning horse's name came to mind — *"Malabar!"* Then he succumbed to a deadly brain fever, learning just before he died that he had won eighty thousand pounds. The story ends with the uncle's sardonic comment to the boy's mother:

> "My God, Hester, you're eighty-odd thousand to the good, and a poor devil of a son to the bad. But, poor devil, poor devil, he's best gone out of a life where he rides his rocking-horse to find a winner."

But if Paul had survived to adulthood, what kind of man would he have become? His parents' excessive spending and his mother's fixation on being both poor and unlucky would most likely have shaped his own view of wealth. Just as no amount of money improved his mother's sense of insufficiency, so he, too, would have let his perceived financial woes make him chronically unhappy. Like his mother, he would have felt "unlucky," especially if he were professionally unsuccessful or had difficulties supporting himself and his family. Perhaps he would have developed a ruinous gambling habit, rolling the dice as well as betting on horses...

And what if this adult version of the "rocking-horse winner" were to walk into your office or work with you virtually? Paul's coaching agenda would probably focus on the following goals:

1. How to increase his wealth.
2. How to become "lucky."
3. How to safeguard his assets.

There is a "generational" dimension to his *Poverty Mindset* that would make it almost impossible to change. In other words, the adult Paul would inherit his limited thinking from his mother, who, in turn, could have inherited it from her parents, grandparents, or even great-grandparents. In addition to his mother's negative influence, his consciousness would also have been shaped by the message reverberating silently through his childhood home: "There must be more money!"

At the end of the coaching engagement, the adult Paul might be pleased with the outcomes; however, you, as coach, would know that there has been no "Ah-ha!" moment, no "*Eureka!*" and no *Epiphany*! You would close his file, having delivered what he requested, but not the "something more" that makes coaching such a life-changing experience.

Polarizing Mindsets

Other polarizing mindsets can manifest in coaching or in any other form of inner guidance. These, like the *Poverty Mindset*, can limit the potential outcomes of the coaching engagement precisely because the client is neither ready nor willing to undergo a mind shift. Take, for example, potential clients who are adherents of conspiracy theories. While it is unlikely that they would seek out coaching, should they do so, the mindset they exemplify could appear unexpectedly in a coaching engagement, especially if they are closet radicals. I suspect, however, that such clients would be "un-coachable" and that an ethical coach would recommend deprogramming instead!

Coachability?

Cynicism aside, rigid thinking is certainly an obstacle to coaching at a deep level. As in the case of a *Poverty Mindset,* one can coach around basic goals and desires, but the possibility of facilitating some kind of *Epiphany* is remote. When the client is convinced that he or she holds the Truth and nothing but the Truth, then formidable megaliths block the path forward. The coach may invite the client to walk around the megaliths, scale them, or dig beneath them — to no avail. This is because the massive stones form an integral part of the client's belief structure and sense of identity; without them, the client is lost existentially and no longer belongs to the "group."

And so it is that our clients cling to their megaliths as if their lives depend upon them. They maintain that they practice the one true religion and that everyone else is damned; they overlook the glaring faults of their political candidates because they have always voted for the same political party; they insist on using old technologies because "they worked in the past"; they accept untrue versions of events — *that African slaves came to America as economic migrants, for example* — because such fantastical tales bolster their flight from reality; and they despise people unlike themselves, especially if they differ in terms of religion, race, ethnicity, socio-economic status, age, gender, sexual orientation, occupation, physical abilities, etc.

Try as we might, there is no moving most megaliths. I think of the monolithic structures I have seen in Malta and the British Isles. Despite the erosion, each towering stone weighs tons, and moving them — whether on sleds or on rollers — would have required coordinated effort and brute force. Someone with a "made-up mind" may learn to modify a few basic behaviors to maintain employment but is not a good candidate for an "Ah-ha!" moment. That client has no intention of letting go of his or her assumptions, outdated strategies, small goals, and limiting beliefs. A first coaching conversation might go something like this:

> **COACH:** "So you would like to focus on how you might organize your neighborhood block so as to reduce crime?"
> **CLIENT:** "Yeah. Not so much to reduce crime but to avoid it happening."
> **COACH:** "Why does this concern you?"
> **CLIENT:** "Well, the city is filled with criminals, illegal aliens, and Black Lives Matter folks. Next, they'll be hitting the suburbs."
> **COACH:** "So you are saying that undocumented immigrants and Black Lives Matter activists are responsible for urban crime?"
> **CLIENT:** "Yeah."
> **COACH:** "And where did you get your information?"
> **CLIENT:** "On Fox News and X — you know, the new Twitter."
> **COACH:** "OK, so if, indeed, these groups are responsible for crime, what might be a non-violent way of deterring them?"
> **CLIENT:** "I'm not interested in deterrents — that'll get us nowhere. They must be stopped."
> **COACH:** "And what do you have in mind?"
> **CLIENT:** "That's why I'm talking to you, but so far, I've come up with gated south suburban villages and armed block militias. I just need to figure out how to fund this and mobilize everyone."
> **COACH:** "I'm afraid that fundraising and community organizing are not my forte. Let me suggest…"

And with that, the coaching conversation comes to a speedy end.

SUMMARY

- *Rigid Mindsets* sabotage both the discovery process and the client's ability to take actionable steps.
- Clients whose minds are already "made up" are basically "un-coachable."
- *Rigid Mindsets* cannot deal with *The Unknown*.
- Limiting beliefs such as a *Poverty Mindset* can pass from one generation to the next or be learned from one's environment.
- Clinging to conspiracy theories is another hallmark of a rigid mindset.
- Clients with a rigid mindset may learn to modify certain behaviors but will resist going deeper.

"Excerpt from 'Nazareth Sequences'"

They do not know,
They have not seen,
They have neither felt
Nor touched nor tasted
The power and glory
Of owning and letting go,
Of being and letting be.
They have not probed
Beneath the skin
For subtle signs of Mystery
Nor studied the harmony
Of opposites
Present in *Yin* and *Yang*,
Animus and *Anima*.

***

They have not heard
Life's rhythms
Pulse beneath the rain-drenched earth
Or whisper in the greening leaves
Of lilacs and magnolias;
They have not smelled its fragrance
Carried by the wind,
Caressed by gentle breezes.
Nor have they felt its beat
Throbbing in the heart of a child.

***

No. They have seen only
Boundaries, barriers
And dichotomies—
Rifts between body and soul,
Man and woman,
Saved and damned,
Divisions wide as gaping canyons,
Bloody as war.

***

They dwell in a crumbling house,
Teetering on termite-ridden frame,
Their resources dwindle in trade,
They lavish wages on refuse
Remembering neither their beginning
Nor their ending,
Nor the days in between,
Neither *Kairos* nor *Chronos*
Nor things of significance.

***

What *they* know
Are limits and restrictions,
Brick walls without doors,
Concrete cells *sans* windows.
For them, life is function,
Rote and predictable,
Their god, Big Brother,
Omniscient, omnipotent,
The feared puppeteer

Who pulls the strings
This way and that,
Jerking obedience
From wooden manikins.

Woman Dreamer, 1989

CHAPTER NINE

Distorted Thinking

"Distorted Thinking" is related to having a *Rigid Mindset* but is not necessarily "rigid" — in other words, clients who exhibit such thinking can often learn to see clearly, provided they are open to change. While a *Rigid Mindset* involves clinging to absolutes, *Distorted Thinking* is more a question of warped perception. I think of shape-shifting mirrors in a Fun House and how disorienting it can be to see oneself widened, elongated, flattened, or reduced in size. At first, the changes may be amusing, but hideous sound effects and hidden exits can soon transform the Fun House into a House of Horrors.

Just as mirrors distort, so our "take" on reality can also be distorted. Looking back on my life, I can recall multiple situations when, for one reason or another, my ability to see was clouded. One of the "lighter" situations involved throwing away an acceptance letter for my first book, a collection of poetry. Having completed *Frost and Fire* in 1984, I never imagined that it would take 75 rejection letters before I found a publisher. In those pre-computer/pre-email days, sending query letters and multiple manuscript submissions was tedious and expensive. Week after week I would head to the post office with stacks of heavy envelopes and, week after week, I would receive an assortment of form letters and somewhat personal letters stating various publishers' regrets. After a while, I would just scan the letters, barely reading the words, before tossing them into the garbage can. I was so demoralized that I lost all energy to write; then, after the arrival of the 75th letter, I went out for a walk to clear my head.

"What *did* that letter say?" I found myself asking. Upon returning home, I retrieved the letter from the wastepaper basket, only to find that it was a letter of acceptance from *Life Enrichment Publishers* in Ohio. My distorted thinking had conditioned me to assume that (a) publishers weren't interested in poetry and (b) I would never find a publisher! At the start of my quest for a publisher, I was both enthusiastic and hopeful; then came the multiple disappointments and the long, long wait for a happy outcome.

The "Teacher Wound"

Sometimes, it's other people's judgments that distort the way we view ourselves and the world around us. As a child, for example, I was not mathematically inclined, possibly because of multiple school changes but more likely because I had an undiagnosed learning disability. My struggle with numbers followed me from school to school, culminating in my failing the 11-Plus, the standardized examination that governed where a child would be admitted to secondary school. We were living in England at the time, and I remember the shock of failure. My friend Josephine did brilliantly, and her place in a school that focused on academic excellence was assured; in contrast, my fate would be to attend a school that specialized in the domestic arts — cooking, sewing, running a household etc.

As it turned out, the external examining board for the 11-Plus gave me a second opportunity to prove myself; it did not go well. I was invited to an interview and, at 11 years of age, found myself standing alone in front of three or four men in dark suits seated in a row behind a long conference table. "Come closer, little girl. There's nothing to be afraid of," said one of the men.

"Why would I be afraid of YOU?" I retorted, not meaning to be rude, but so terrified that I said the first thing that came to mind.

I don't recall much else about the interview except one of the examiners asked if I had a favorite TV program. Had I mentioned one of David Attenborough's documentaries or some other cultural program, the outcome might have been different; instead, I blurted out that my favorite show was an American sitcom, *Father of the Bride*. Evidently, that failed to impress the examiners, for my parents were notified of my failure shortly afterward. Josephine may have been university material, but I clearly was not. Happily, we returned to Malta when the school year ended. While no mention of the 11-Plus results surfaced at my new school, I held the conviction that I was less intelligent than my classmates and would never do well academically. It would be three years before I could move beyond this negative self-concept, and only then because I finally had a teacher who believed in me — and helped me believe in myself.

Under Miss Wood's tutelage, at the age of 14, I went from believing the lie that I was "useless" to realizing that I could design my own life. Not only did I develop a passion for history and archaeology but I also ended up running the drama club (and writing and producing plays!), editing the school magazine, starting the debating society, and chairing the school charity drive. In my last two years — Sixth Form — I also served as Head Girl (School Captain), while carrying a formidable load of A-Level subjects to qualify for university. Throughout my academic career, whenever I have had non-performing students in class, it has invariably been because of some lie they have believed about themselves. In most cases, many have carried what could be described as a *"Teacher Wound"* for years — perhaps since kindergarten or earlier. Whether a teacher shamed them in front of the entire class, slashed their assignments with red ink, or else made derogatory comments to them in private, the effect has been the same: to make them feel that they are not "enough" and to believe that they are doomed to a lifetime of failure and few options.

Lost Potential

Sadly, many of those who end up with poor academic records have the greatest potential. Take, for example, the student who, by sophomore year, was labeled a troublemaker because he asked questions his teachers couldn't answer. With an IQ of 157, he was bored out of his mind and ended up dropping out of a well-regarded Jesuit high school. He, too, assumed he was not "college material" until he was miraculously admitted to a private university — albeit on probation — despite having a Grade Point Average (GPA) of 2.00 out of a possible perfect score of 4.00. In his first semester, he not only made the dean's list but was also invited to take graduate courses in philosophy to stimulate conversation; there, he shone and even considered going on to graduate school — until he discovered that his professors were quoting from books *he* had read, and they hadn't. His second *Epiphany* was to see through the façade of academic posturing and to want no part of it.

So much harm can be done in the name of education. The child who feels like a misfit at school or considers himself or herself to be "dumb" will likely carry this distorted thinking into other aspects of life, from relationships to work. Highly-gifted students, students with learning disabilities, students who are audio-visual learners, students who speak English as a second language, or who start school without any knowledge of the language of instruction are all disadvantaged in the typical classroom. This is also true of minority students who may not only have to deal with discrimination but also lack the cultural framework to make sense of the material covered in class, in textbooks, or even in standardized testing.

Threshold of Adventure

In the archetypal *Hero Quest*, the demons most likely to block the path forward across the *Threshold of Adventure* are the demons of *Distorted Thinking*. In some cases, these "demons" may represent the concerns of well-meaning or overprotective friends and relatives. The would-be heroes are poised to go on some grand adventure or launch an exciting career when someone attempts to dissuade them:

> *"You know, darling, you have always been sickly — don't you think going to India would be inviting trouble?"* **OR**
> *"Why on earth would you want to go back to school at your age — you will never keep up with all those youngsters!"* **OR**
> *"Starting your own business is simply too risky — besides, we need you here at the family restaurant!"*

In other cases, the demonic voices are not well-intentioned at all but have one goal only: to prevent would-be heroes from stepping over the *Threshold of Adventure* by using fear tactics:

> *"You don't have what it takes to be CEO — you won't last a week when they see how inept you really are!"* **OR**
> *"There have been avalanches all winter — you'd be a fool to go snowboarding there!"* **OR**
> *"Run for office at your age? No one will vote for you!"*

Utterances like these are designed to keep would-be *Heroes* small and unfulfilled. They plant seeds of doubt, eroding confidence, destroying dreams, and stunting the growth and development of their victims. Worst of all, however, is when these demonic voices invade the would-be heroes' own psyches, taking possession of their thoughts:

"I don't have what it takes." **OR**
"I'm too old." **OR**
"I'm too young." **OR**
"I don't have enough money." **OR**
"I'll never be successful." **OR**
"I don't have the credentials." **OR**
"I'm not smart enough." **OR**
"I can't survive on my own."

I Can't Because XXX

Sadly, *Distorted Thinking* shows up with regularity in coaching sessions. Clients come in (or sign on!) who profess to want to change their lives but who seem to have little enthusiasm or energy to do so. In fact, their very aura feels dark and cumbersome. It doesn't take long before we begin to hear the distorting scripts they live by — the *False-Self Narratives* if you will, that keep them from making progress. Some can't find the courage to leave a toxic relationship because they doubt whether they can survive being single or because they don't believe anyone will find them lovable. Others stay in entry-level positions or jobs they find boring because they are afraid to leave their comfort zones. Still others continually make excuses to explain why they will not take "the road less traveled," even if they find it inviting.

The mantra, *"I can't because XXX,"* is so firmly implanted in their brains that even setting an agenda is tough. Fear paralyzes them from dreaming, from imagining, from desiring; all they can see is what they know — and this is why they are chronically unhappy! The "good news" is that their unhappiness can become the portal through which change happens. Unlike *Rigid Thinkers*, those who suffer from *Distorted Thinking* are more willing to let go of their limiting beliefs and to be open to new insights. The challenge for the coach is to help such clients "re-write" the distorted narratives that have controlled their lives.

This usually involves tracing the narrative to its starting point, not in a therapeutic way, but through a direct question or series of questions that can expose the lies they have believed. Here is an excerpt from a coaching session that reflects this coaching strategy:

> **COACH:** "What I'm hearing is that you intend to turn down this job offer because you don't feel qualified for it."
> **CLIENT:** "Yeah."
> **COACH:** "But you have all the experience the job description requires!"
> **CLIENT:** "True, but that was in a family-owned company — perhaps they were just doing me a favor by employing me."
> **COACH:** "How long did you work there?"
> **CLIENT:** "About ten years — until COVID."
> **COACH:** "And what kind of performance feedback did you receive?"
> **CLIENT:** "Well, all the performance reviews led to raises and promotions. When the company folded because of the pandemic, I was handling most of the major accounts."
> **COACH:** "So what does that tell you?"
> **CLIENT:** "Well, they trusted me, but, again, I was the son of the CEO."
> **COACH:** "I'm curious as to why you believe your success in the company was just because your dad was CEO. Where's that coming from?"
> **CLIENT:** "Working for Applegate was my first job, right out of college. I was a 'C' student and couldn't even get into grad school — at least, not the schools I wanted to attend. The military turned me down because I had flat feet, and my only job offers before Applegate were for non-skilled workers. That hardly showed potential!"
> **COACH:** "Tell me about those 'C' grades."

CLIENT: "I hated college. I went from a small private school where I was an 'A' student — valedictorian, in fact — to an enormous state school with 100+ students in every class. The faculty were more into research than teaching, and I could tell they felt bothered whenever I went to see them during office hours. I began to fall behind — didn't even hand in my assignments at times, even though I had stayed up all night working on them. I flunked a couple of classes and ended up having to re-take them just to graduate."

COACH: "Hmmm. So you were an 'A' student in high school and then became a 'C' student in college. What does that tell you?"

CLIENT: "That I wasn't cut out for college."

COACH: "Really? Let's re-frame this. Can you complete the following sentence: I was a 'C' student in college because…"

CLIENT: "I was a 'C' student in college because I failed to hand in my homework."

COACH: "And?"

CLIENT: "And because I was bored."

COACH: "And?"

CLIENT: "And because my instructors weren't interested in teaching."

COACH: "And?"

CLIENT: "And because I didn't receive the help I needed."

COACH: "And?"

CLIENT: "And because I was overwhelmed by the size of the school."

COACH: "So how do you feel about that 'C' now?"

CLIENT: "OK, so it doesn't define me, but I still don't feel qualified for this new position."

COACH: "Let's try another re-framing. Instead of saying you had a successful career at Applegate because you were the CEO's son, what might you say instead?"

CLIENT: "That's more challenging."
COACH: "Give it a try."
CLIENT: "I initially got the job because no one else would hire me—"
COACH: "Go on."
CLIENT: "And at first, people said I was just there because of my dad."
COACH: "But then?"
CLIENT: "But then they began to respect me because I was pulling my weight — and not only that, but I cut costs and brought in new clients."
COACH: "Go on."
CLIENT: "That's why I got the great performance reviews, raises, and even bonuses."
COACH: "And?"
CLIENT: "OK, I can see where you're going with this. Perhaps you can help walk me through the pros and cons of this new position."
COACH: "I would be delighted to!"

SUMMARY

- *Distorted Thinking* sabotages both the discovery process and taking actionable steps.
- Warped perceptions about the self often originate with other people's negative judgments.
- Clients who suffered a *Teacher Wound* in childhood often suffer from feelings of inadequacy and perform poorly in school.
- Feelings of "being dumb" carry over into relationships and professional life.
- "Demons" of *Distorted Thinking* interrupt the archetypal *Hero's Quest* to which each person is called. These demons can be external or internal.

"On the Stupidity of Gulls"

There they stand and sit
On the bird-splashed feathered tarmac,
Comfortable on the grass ridges
Separating parking lanes,
One from the other,
Looking straight ahead
Towards the sands.
Motionless, they observe the sea
As though assessing some Promised Land
And finding it wanting.
Around them,
Cars circle, swerve,
Sometimes smashing heads and wings,
Plastering bits of flesh
To whitewalls,
But the stubborn gulls stay,
Unruffled,
Staring at the beckoning water.

Extraordinary Time, 1988

CHAPTER TEN

Primary Addictions

It takes self-awareness and maturity to recognize our *Primary Addictions* — that is, those unconscious beliefs and desires that drive our less noble attitudes and behaviors. At a conscious level, most of us are aware of our more visible addictions, such as the ones that are supported by consuming alcohol, food, and drugs or by engaging in excessive shopping, gambling, watching TV, or interacting with social media. These visible addictions are usually apparent to those we live and work with, and even if we are in denial, soon there is no hiding the fact that we have a problem. This is especially true when our addictions begin to have an impact on our work and our relationships. Warnings, threats, and ultimatums are often the catalyst for seeking help — not in coaching but in therapy or Twelve Step Programs such as *Alcoholics Anonymous*.

But let's return to what I referred to as *"Primary Addictions."* These addictions cannot be detected by empty alcohol bottles, drained bank accounts, or closets overflowing with unworn clothing and countless pairs of shoes. There is nothing to "hide" because, without self-reflection, addicts are usually completely unaware that they have an addictive mindset. This mindset can manifest in the *Distorted Thinking* and *False-Self Narratives* that I addressed in previous chapters, but it goes deeper, colors the addict's whole personality, and can be more difficult to detect.

In his great mystical poem, *The Conference of the Birds*, the twelfth-century Sufi poet, Farid Ud-Din Attar, presents an allegory of the spiritual journey. Led by the Hoopoe, the birds of the world set out to find their ideal king — the Simorgh. To reach him, however, they must undertake a perilous journey through seven terrible valleys. This is no mere geographical journey but a stripping of all their *Primary Addictions*. In seeking the Truth, the birds must face their own truth and submit to the flame of purgation; only then will they be able to complete their journey to the Simorgh.

The beauty of this poem is that it presents universal "vices" (*Primary Addictions*) through the birds' own experiences. Having committed to embarking on *The Way*, each bird suddenly has a change of heart and reluctantly declines the invitation. Evidently, the thought of renouncing the ego-self is simply too terrifying. The birds' excuses help readers identify their own limiting mindsets through the safety of the allegory; there is no need to wallow in shame or despair because the protagonists are only make-believe birds, even if their sins are recognizable. We can laugh at the birds and pity them; at the same time, we can "confess" to each other that we identify with the Owl, the Nightingale or even the Finch, without having to spill out all our "dirty laundry." But let's meet some of these birds and imagine how we might interact with them in a coaching context.

The Nightingale: Addicted to Falling in Love

First in Attar's allegory comes the Nightingale, who knows the secrets of all love. Infatuated with the Rose, the Nightingale is so drowned in love that he only wants to worship her. The Rose alone is all he can think about; the quest for her is his reality. At first, one might be tempted to sympathize with the Nightingale. After all, anyone who has ever fallen in love surely remembers the early days of wanting nothing more than to be in the presence of their beloved. If we look at the Nightingale's words, however, some red flags surface. The Rose, apparently, blooms only for the Nightingale: "Her buds are mine; she blossoms in my sight" (Attar, p.46). So all-encompassing is his love that if the Rose should disappear, the Nightingale admits he would lose his reason and no longer be able to sing: "How could I leave her for a single night?" (Attar, p.46).

The Nightingale's *Primary Addiction* is possessive love. For him, the Rose is the object of his desire, the reason for his existence, the source of his bliss. This is not a healthy relationship but one of mutual dependency, with the Rose serving as the object and the Nightingale as the subject. The Hoopoe is quick to denounce this superficial love and to point out that all beauty is transient. "Forget the rose's blush and blush for shame!" he says as he urges the Nightingale to prepare his wings for the great quest to find the Simorgh.

Nightingales are most likely to appear in life coaching and couple's coaching. As in the case of Attar's Nightingale, the Nightingales we coach soon give themselves away just by their speech. Unable to be away from their partners, they are quick to inform us that separation means death. The lyrics of Harry Nilsson's, *I Can't Live*, come to mind: "Can't live if living is without you/Can't live, can't give any more/Can't live, can't give any more...."

I remember belting this song out as a teenager, passionately believing every single word and that life without one's heartthrob was not worth living. My only excuse is that since the human brain doesn't develop until age 25, I was clearly unable to think as an adult. But going back to coaching, Nightingales often reveal themselves by their choice of pronouns — for example, "*my* marriage" instead of "*our* marriage" or "*my* house" instead of "*our* house." Though they profess to love their partners, Nightingales tend to see their significant others as extensions of themselves or even as "pets" or small children needing protection.

I think of Henrik Ibsen's play, *A Doll's House*, in which Torvald Helmer treats his wife, Nora, like one of the children. She is "acceptable" as long as she behaves according to his expectations, but as soon as he discovers that she took out a loan without his permission and that she forged her father's signature on the promissory note, his rage knows no bounds. Even though the loan was to finance a trip to Italy so that Torvald could regain his health, he can only think about how Nora's actions threaten his position and reputation. In an instant, Nora goes from being his "most treasured possession" to becoming a "wretched woman." And, in an instant, Nora has a profound *Epiphany*: Torvald was never actually in love with her but thought it was "fun" to be in love with her. This insight leads to her departure from his house and to the slammed door that marks the end of the play.

Nightingales often seek out coaching because they are experiencing problems in their relationships. They may hire a coach on their own or engage a coach with their partner who, unbeknownst to them, may either be a fragile Rose or another Nightingale. Since "Couples Coaching" sounds more socially acceptable than "Couples Counseling," they are more likely to hire a coach than a therapist. Moreover, they seldom recognize that the difficulties they are experiencing with their significant other stem from addictive love. Instead, they are often perplexed by their partner's unhappiness or fail to recognize that love, taken to extremes, can be suffocating.

It may take a few sessions before the coach realizes that the couple has a deeper set of problems than disagreements over finances, child raising, or dealing with in-laws. Suddenly, these generic-sounding issues take on a more personal dimension:

"You love your parents more than you love me." **OR**
"You pay more attention to the kids than to me." **OR**
"If you worked from home, we could have a better sex life." **OR**
"How am I supposed to have a life when you travel so much for work?" **OR**
"Why should I delay starting a new career because we constantly have to move?"

The coach then has a few options:

To mirror back what is being said.

1. To allow the "Rose" to have a voice.
2. To explore how both parties might work on personal development.
3. To help both parties redefine what "Love" means to them, individually and collectively.
4. To renegotiate the contract to include the newly identified issues.
5. To refer to a therapist.

For the relationship to be "saved," both parties need clarity regarding the emotional drama in which they play starring roles — and both need to be willing to change!

The Hawk: Addicted to Power

One bird that is likely to appear in corporate coaching and leadership coaching is the Hawk. Like many executives, Attar's Hawk is a braggart whose talk is stuffed with "armies, glory, kings" (p.55). What Hawks value the most are connections, especially with those of high rank. They stop at nothing to put themselves in the orbit of the rich and famous, using flattery and name-dropping to make themselves noticeable. For Hawks, greatness does not consist of accomplishing great deeds but establishing and maintaining their proximity to those in high places:

"A seed/From my great sovereign's hand is all I need;/ The eminence I have suffices me./I cannot travel; I would rather be/Perched on the royal wrist than struggling through/Some arid wadi with no end in view" (p.55).

The Hoopoe calls out the Hawk for being superficial but also provides a stark warning: a courtier's fate depends upon the king's whim, and destruction can strike at any hour:

> "Distance yourself from kings and worldly power./ A king is like a raging fire, men say;/The wisest conduct is to keep away" (p.56).

How many leaders end up in coaching because their "king" has either fallen from grace or left the firm? And how many leaders suddenly discover that the CEO's patronage is insufficient to guarantee employment, especially when budgets become tight? Instead of building skills, Hawks often invest their time and energy into cultivating friendships with important people, imagining that this will secure their careers. At the same time, they tend to disassociate themselves from their colleagues, especially those of a lower rank or those who tend to be viewed as minor players. Attar's Hawk admits, "The ecstasy my sovereign brings/Has turned my gaze from vulgar company" (p.55). What he fails to understand is that a colleague he despises for being "vulgar" may one day be elevated to his supervisor — or may have the connections to help him when he is searching for new employment.

A trend in the corporate world — at least, in those companies with high employee satisfaction — is the concept of "servant leadership." Simply put, this means that instead of authoritarian management, leaders share decision-making, invite feedback, and cultivate collegiality while exhibiting empathy, understanding, and dedication. Instead of running the corporation remotely, with little or no input from their subordinates, "servant leaders" are concerned with all their stakeholders — executive officers, human resource professionals, marketing specialists, entry-level employees, support staff, interns, vendors, clients, and so forth. Such leaders distrust the flatterers and name-droppers in their midst; instead, they reward authenticity, integrity, and hard work, letting it be known that there is no room for favoritism in the workplace. On its homepage, *GreatPlacetoWork.com* states: "While some leaders may believe it isn't possible to prioritize both profits and employee satisfaction, the 100 Best Companies prove that employee experience is not only compatible with profitability — it's vital to achieving fiscal goals." Hawks have no place in such companies.

Hawks seek out coaching when their old strategies cease to work. For example, they may have a new boss with whom they cannot get along; or there may be a new hire who threatens their position because of his or her exceptional experience and qualifications, or they may discover they are about to be laid off and are in a panic as to "next steps."

Perceiving themselves to be loyal, Hawks have difficulty accepting their fall from grace. They have been supportive to a fault and, always discrete, have served as confidants; they have placed their leaders' wishes and whims above their own — and sometimes, above what is ethical. They have flattered and defended, sacrificing their integrity for the sake of some VP or CEO who has now conveniently forgotten them.

Listening to this saga, the coach needs to express empathy while creating that safe environment in which the client can unload complex feelings, hurt, and resentments. Only then can coach and client begin to explore new strategies that reflect the client's authentic self.

The Duck: Addicted to the Status Quo

When "Ducks" seek coaching, it is usually because their jobs depend upon it or because they have already experienced a shift in consciousness, albeit a minor one. Attar's Duck is addicted to her own perfection and to the comfort of her pond. Believing herself to be "the purest bird that ever flew or swam," this Duck has no desire to venture further than her sanctuary — her pond — and is completely opposed to traversing arid deserts: "Water's the only home I've ever known;/Why should I care about the Simorgh's throne?" She is much like employees (or CEOs!) who have performed well in the same environment for years but who are completely risk-averse, inflexible, and unwilling to adapt. Resisting all new policies and technologies, the Duck insists on doing things her way as she has always done, until she sees the handwriting on the wall — or on a pink slip!

The wise Hoopoe points out, "Your life is passed/In vague aquatic dreams which cannot last/A sudden wave and they are swept away" (p.51). Very often, it is a "sudden wave" that forces the Duck to reconsider her obstinate mindset; she is either placed on notice or else is let go from her position, and, either way, she knows she must adapt or perish!

But having a Duck nature is not just limited to individuals. At the corporate level, some companies fail to innovate and therefore crash — a prime example being Kodak. So secure was Kodak as the global leader of the film photography business that it failed to respond adequately to the disruptions of the digital age. In his article, *Kodak's Downfall Wasn't About Technology* (Web. *Harvard Review,* July 15, 2016), Scott D. Anthony points out that Kodak did, in fact, invest in digital technologies; however, the emphasis remained on "business as usual". "Kodak created a digital camera, invested in the technology, and even understood that photos would be shared online. Where the company failed was in not realizing that online photo sharing *was* the new business, not just a way to expand the printing business" (https://hbr.org/2016/07/kodaks-downfall-wasnt-about-technology).

Anthony concludes by stating that Kodak's downfall was a case of lost potential, for despite having the talent and money, the corporation: "ended up the victim of the aftershocks of a disruptive change."

The same could be said of Blockbuster, which, in its heyday, had 9000 video rental stores globally, each offering thousands of titles. Like Kodak, however, Blockbuster rested on its laurels, failing to see the threat of two major competitors — Netflix and Redbox. By the time it canceled its unpopular practice of charging late fees and moved into streaming videos, it was too late. According to *Business Insider*, only one Blockbuster has survived, but this has been because of innovation. Based in Oregon, it has partnered with Airbnb, attracting tourists who wish to reminisce about the former global giant!

But Blockbuster and Kodak were not the only corporations that notoriously missed the moment: Blackberry and Nokia failed to adapt to changing phone technology; Toys R Us and other retailers underestimated the power of online shopping; Pan Am, once "the world's most experienced airline" failed to adapt to deregulation; Borders Books didn't anticipate the meteoric rise of Amazon; newspapers were too slow in moving from print to digital formats. These companies soon lost their market share, were forced into bankruptcy, or disappeared altogether.

Sadly, the same fate awaited small business owners who clung to old ways of production, distribution, and marketing. For example, photographers who resisted the shift from film cameras to digital cameras; or travel agents who were taken by surprise when their former customers began booking through Expedia, or CheapOair; or neighborhood restaurants that underestimated the McDonalds' phenomenon; or advertisers that continued to use cold calling and print phone directories even as Google key ad words were transforming advertising…

Through coaching, Ducks can find the courage to explore the worlds beyond their ponds. While affirming all that Ducks love about their pristine habitats, coaches can help them explore possible disadvantages or "weak spots" that might lead to their destruction. Questions might include:

"What might your competitors be working on while you are enjoying what you have already built?" **OR**
"What internal threats may there be if your company is no longer innovating?" **OR**
"Why might it be necessary to incorporate AI into your company?" **OR**
"If your company had a reputation for being cutting-edge 20 years ago, what is its reputation now?"

Such questions begin to puncture a Duck's complacency and provide a foundation for moving forward.

The Finch: Addicted to Fear

Finches, like Ducks, are risk-averse and prefer to maintain the *status quo* rather than explore new options. Terrified of anything unfamiliar, Finches would rather stay put in challenging situations than start over. Far from being drawn to "the road less traveled," they prefer the "well-worn path," using every excuse to justify staying home. Attar's timid Finch is quick to use her physical weakness as an excuse to avoid the journey: She is "less sturdy than a hair," and her feathers are "too weak" to carry her. Moreover, she not only claims to be too sickly to stand before the Simorgh's throne, but she also points to her lack of courage as proof of her unworthiness. All this enrages the Hoopoe who sees through her hypocrisy: "You teasing little bird/ This humble ostentation is absurd!" (p.60).

Finches are to be found in every kind of coaching situation. Addicted to fear, they may claim that they are planning on making some dramatic changes in their lives, but, in reality, they present excuse after excuse for not doing so. Coaching conversations often follow this pattern:

> "I want to quit my job, BUT..."; "I want to confront my colleague, BUT..."; "I want to go back to school, BUT..."; "I want to relocate, BUT..."; "I want to start dating again, BUT..."; "I want to re-structure the company, BUT..."; "I want to hire more support staff, BUT..."; "I want to diversify our inventory, BUT..."; "I want to take up martial arts, BUT...", and so forth.

There is always an excuse, and when that excuse proves unfounded, there is another one, and yet another...

Finches are so terrified that change will bring negative consequences that they miss out on professional and personal opportunities, preferring limitation and even abuse to facing the unknown. They would rather stay in a toxic relationship or work environment than leave because they fear repeating the same mistakes or feel they don't deserve anything better. Worse still, they hold others back from making positive changes as well — their colleagues, their significant others, even their children. The only way forward for Finches is to see that the "BUTs" they present are unfounded and that taking "next steps" is safer than taking no steps at all. Such *Epiphanies* do not come without a struggle.

Not surprisingly, Finches do not do well when they are criticized, challenged, or put down — or where too much is asked of them! Aware of this, the coach needs to establish a safe environment in which the Finch feels free to share shame, failures, embarrassment, and feelings of inadequacy. Without delving into therapy (which some Finches definitely need), the coach might use imaginative strategies to help clients move beyond their limitations. For example, the coach might invite a Finch to draw a picture of the new home he is too afraid to purchase or of the partner she hopes to attract. Or the coach might suggest that the Finch design a job description for his or her "ideal job." Using play puts Finch clients at ease and reinforces their self-worth because there are no "right or wrong" answers.

Other Birds

So far, we have looked only at the Nightingale, the Hawk, the Duck, and the Finch, but the other birds also need to uncover their hidden liabilities. *Primary Addictions* stop us from being our best selves; however, Attar's birds initially consider their vices to be virtues. The Nightingale flaunts his skills as a lover, not realizing that possessive love is simply a manifestation of narcissism. For his part, the Hawk is proud of his connections to people in high places, unaware that he is a sycophant living vicariously through others' status. Both the Duck and the Finch reject change for different reasons: the Duck because of her elevated sense of self and the Finch because of her self-abasement and fear. But these are not the only character flaws that can block growth. The pretty Parrot, for example, thinks she is God's gift to humanity, while the Partridge is addicted to jewels, the Homa sees himself as a "kingmaker," the melancholy Heron is obsessed with the past, and the Owl seeks gold and despises humanity.

Like the Hoopoe, we can laugh at these birds, mocking their delusions and marveling at their materialism. If we probe a little deeper, however, we might notice that we, too, share in their imperfections — the same imperfections our clients struggle with, even if they have yet to recognize this. If you are open to a playful exploration of your own *Primary Addictions*, I invite you to take the *Quiz for the Birds*, a non-scientific character assessment based on *The Conference of the Birds*. I developed this quiz many years ago when teaching *Myths, Signs, and Symbols* at DePaul University, and since then

I have used it with countless classes and retreat groups — with great success! If you are not up to a little introspection right now, then feel free to bypass the quiz and go to the next chapter!

Quiz for the Birds:

Each of the birds listed below is about to embark on a spiritual quest, but each has a character flaw that blocks acceptance of the journey. To see with which bird you identify the most closely, answer the following questions as truthfully as you can by circling either "True" or "False." Then add up your TRUE scores; if scores tie, choose the profile that seems the best fit. Please note that the "Hoopoe" is the perfect spiritual leader, so even if this is your highest score, work with a bird that has some character deficiencies!

THE HOOPOE

1. You are a natural leader, able to inspire and motivate others.
   True   False

2. You have a history of valiant exploits.
   True   False

3. You exhort others to reach their spiritual and moral potential.
   True   False

4. You are not afraid to offer honest critiques of others' motives and behaviors.
   True   False

5. You see things clearly, beneath the surface.
   True   False

6. You understand the mystical dimension of things.
   True   False

7. You are single-hearted in your quest for *Truth*.
   True   False

8. You are skilled at practicing self-discipline.
   True   False

9. Others regard you as a spiritual leader.
   True   False

10. You practice what you preach.
    True   False

Score:
Primary Addiction: None

THE NIGHTINGALE

1. You are prone to invest most of your energy in significant relationships.
   True   False

2. You cannot live without your significant other.
   True   False

3. Broken relationships cause you to pine away.
   True   False

4. The one you love exists for you alone.
   True   False

5. To be apart from your significant other is intolerable.
   True   False

6. To be in love is what gives life meaning.
   True   False

7. You know the secrets of all love.
   True   False

8. You are content to be Love's Fool.
   True   False

9. You write love poetry on a regular basis.
   True   False

10. Without you, your beloved would die of grief.
    True   False

Score:
Primary Addiction: Cloying love.

THE PARROT

1. Liberty means being free from rules, cages, and oppressive people.
   True   False

2. You take pride in your appearance.
   True   False

3. Others are envious of your exotic looks.
   True   False

4. People like to be around you because they enjoy looking at you.
   True   False

5. You judge others according to appearances.
   True   False

6. Others tend to judge you by the way you look.
   True   False

7. You like friends who appreciate your exotic ways.
   True   False

8. You are not like ordinary mortals.
   True   False

9. You are too beautiful merely to be on display.
   True   False

10. Your external assets make you superior to others.
    True   False

Score:
Primary Addiction: Vanity

THE PEACOCK

1. Heaven means a return to a former state of bliss that has now passed.
   True   False

2. You blame others for your fall from grace.
   True   False

3. Your creator took special joy in creating you.
   True   False

4. You are not to blame for your transgressions.
   True   False

5. You are content with immediate gratification.
   True   False

6. You have no desire for self-improvement.
   True   False

7. A palace now is preferable to eternal reward.
   True   False

8. You are entitled to special treatment.
   True   False

9. You are not like ordinary mortals.
   True   False

10. You are easily taken in by flattery.
    True   False

Score:
Primary Addiction: Sense of Superiority

THE DUCK

1. You are so comfortable in your present element that you would prefer not to leave it.
   True   False

2. Your spiritual practices depend upon maintaining your present way of life.
   True   False

3. You take pride in your way of life.
   True   False

4. You practice your religion scrupulously.
   True   False

5. Prayer makes you immune to temptation.
   True   False

6. Being perfect is what is most important in life.
   True   False

7. Your home is an extension of who you are.
   True   False

8. You can only be your real self in your environment.
   True   False

9. To live alone in perfection is heaven to you.
   True   False

10. Other people are sinful in comparison to you.
    True   False

Score:
Primary Addiction: Comfort, being "Holier than Thou"

THE PARTRIDGE

1. Your main goal in life is to make money.
   True   False

2. You like collecting treasures of different kinds.
   True   False

3. Beautiful objects improve your quality of life.
   True   False

4. Hunting for rare and beautiful objects gives life meaning.
   True   False

5. You go to great lengths to protect your possessions.
   True   False

6. You are afraid that others might steal your treasures.
   True   False

7. You enjoy cleaning and polishing your treasures.
   True   False

8. You are always looking for ways of acquiring more.
   True   False

9. What you own pretty much defines you.
   True   False

10. Your treasures keep you from wanting to leave home.
    True   False

Score:
Primary Addiction: Materialism/Hoarding

THE HOMA

1. You take great pleasure in social status.
   True   False

2. You enjoy exerting influence over others.
   True   False

3. Others seek your company to share your status.
   True   False

4. Your friendship can make a difference to people who want to get ahead.
   True   False

5. You have little time for ordinary mortals.
   True   False

6. Others are fortunate to have your endorsement.
   True   False

7. You are aware of your power and enjoy asserting it.
   True   False

8. Many people are indebted to you for their successes.
   True   False

9. You do not need superiors of any kind.
   True   False

10. You are a gift to humanity.
    True   False

Score:
Primary Addiction: Power and Influence

THE HAWK

1. You are content to assist those in leadership positions and to let their glory reflect on you.
   True   False

2. Knowing those in high places is important to you.
   True   False

3. You take pride in name-dropping.
   True   False

4. Others judge you by those you know.
   True   False

5. You know how to please your superiors.
   True   False

6. You exercise tact and restraint to stay in favor.
   True   False

7. You see everything but say nothing.
   True   False

8. Your greatest joy is having an elevated position.
   True   False

9. You turn your back on family and friends who are inferior.
   True   False

10. You play the game to be socially acceptable.
    True   False

Score:
Primary Addiction: Flattery and Importance

THE HERON

1. There is a strong nostalgic side to you that keeps you focusing on the past.
   True   False

2. You are mournful by temperament.
   True   False

3. You have a tendency towards depression.
   True   False

4. You constantly dwell on happier times.
   True   False

5. You prefer solitude to companionship.
   True   False

6. You are more comfortable with the surface than with the depths.
   True   False

7. You love what is unattainable.
   True   False

8. Sometimes, you wallow in self-pity.
   True   False

9. You prefer to love from a distance than to risk the real thing.
   True   False

10. Your goals tend to be superficial.
    True   False

Score:
Primary Addiction: Nostalgia, Melancholy

THE OWL

1. You dream of winning the lottery.
   True   False

2. You find humanity despicable.
   True   False

3. You seek tranquility in isolation.
   True   False

4. You are preoccupied with finding buried treasure.
   True   False

5. People tend to let you down.
   True   False

6. You dream of acquiring great wealth.
   True   False

7. You can never have enough money.
   True   False

8. You have fantasies about getting rich.
   True   False

9. Any wealth you might have is for your own use only.
   True   False

10. You must guard your possessions from greedy people.
    True   False

Score:
Primary Addiction: Greed, Inability to Share

THE FINCH

1. You are unworthy of any great adventures.
   True   False

2. The thought of adventures makes you feel weak.
   True   False

3. You lack the courage to embark on any quest.
   True   False

4. Others are stronger and more courageous than you.
   True   False

5. Ill health holds you back from the journey.
   True   False

6. You are unworthy of entering into the Divine Presence.
   True   False

7. You need to preserve your strength for ordinary tasks.
   True   False

8. God's gaze would reduce you to ashes.
   True   False

9. You are content to remain in the safety of your home.
   True   False

10. Others are more worthy of the journey.
    True   False

Score:
Primary Addiction: Fear, Poor Self-Esteem

Once you know your "bird score," reflect on how you manifest this bird in daily life. Going back over your history, from your first memories to the present, explore whether any patterns have now become visible. This can be a painful, humbling journey, but the awareness itself is the first antidote to healing. On a personal note, the first time I read *The Conference of the Birds*, I knew immediately that I was a Nightingale — and that I always had been! As a toddler, I became excessively attached to dolls, stuffed animals, and anyone who showed me affection of any kind. When I left Rosebud at *La Tour Eiffel*, for example, I wept so profusely in the car that my parents drove back to Paris to look for her — to no avail! And when a beautiful porcelain doll replaced the yellow duster I then used as a security blanket, I was inconsolable. This new "Rosebud" could open and close her eyes and say "Mamma," but she lacked the warmth and softness of the yellow duster. Fast forward to goldfish, terrapins, friendships, and relationships, and the same pattern of emotional attachment showed up with regularity. Working through this pattern has been an ongoing challenge, but present-tense awareness has saved me from pining away any further!

If you take this quiz with a group, see if there are any others who identify with the same bird; small "bird-based" discussions can be both enlightening and comforting. At the end of small group sharing, hearing some of the discoveries each group has made is fascinating. *Do I use this quiz with clients?* Occasionally — it depends upon the client! As with my other "tools," this is a resource that heightens my intuition and awareness but does not necessarily need to be shared.

SUMMARY

- *Primary Addictions* are usually invisible to both clients and their coaches.
- These addictions are powerful saboteurs on the journey to wholeness.
- They prevent us from making life-giving choices.
- Each of the birds in Attar's allegory, *The Conference of the Birds*, has a primary addiction, for example vanity, greed, power-lust.
- The "coach approach" to *Primary Addictions* is to mirror back what is being said, with patience, empathy and non-judgment, asking questions that coach in the direction of authenticity.
- Sometimes, the *Primary Addiction* is so deep-rooted and so destructive that a referral to therapy may be in order.

"Dry Wood"

I am whittled away
Like dry wood
Under a skilled carver's knife,
Trimmed of superfluities,
Pared to the core.
The shavings of my life
Lie at my feet
And I stand strangely naked
Beneath the singing blade
Which strips, refines
Gives form,
Leaving me quivering
Like a thing newborn.

Extraordinary Time, 1988

CHAPTER ELEVEN

That Terrifying Shadow

The term *"Shadow"* brings up a variety of connotations. For some, J. M. Barrie's much-beloved story of *Peter Pan* comes to mind. In this narrative, the protagonist accidentally loses his shadow until Wendy sews it back on, an action that suggests this shadow is part of Peter's identity. For others, *The Shadow* is synonymous with sin, but this implies that it is evil and must be "conquered" if one hopes to attain holiness. Photographers, in contrast, see both the challenges and advantages of shadows. Unwanted shadows can ruin portraits and landscapes alike, but with the right lens and manual camera settings, the contrast between light and darkness can create amazingly dramatic effects. Then, of course, there is the Jungian theory of *The Shadow*.

Although I have explored *False-Self Narratives, Distorted Thinking, Rigid Mindsets,* and *Primary Addictions* under separate headings, they all emerge from the same place: from that unconscious part of ourselves that began forming in the womb, from the first moment we were able to absorb our mother's fear, anger, grief, despair... Yes, though there are few scientific studies on the topic, through my own observations and conversations with other parents, clients, and psychologists, I have concluded that *The Shadow* begins to develop pre-birth when we absorb maternal emotions — good, bad, and neutral — through chemical signals via the placenta (*ScienceDaily*). As a result of such maternal influences, it seems that a newborn can be pre-disposed to feel either wanted, loved, and safe or unwanted, unloved, and unsafe. If this is true, then there are implications not only for individuals who may be struggling to understand their psychological makeup but also for generations born in war zones, in repressive regimes, or during times of famine or natural disasters. Fascinating as it may be, however, this topic lies beyond the scope of my work on *Epiphany Moments* in coaching.

The Personal Unconscious versus the Collective Unconscious

For Carl G. Jung, "the contents of the personal unconscious are acquired during the individual's lifetime" (as opposed to pre-birth), and it is there that the personal *Shadow* resides until we acquire self-knowledge by recognizing the "dark aspects" of our personalities (Campbell, p.145). My use of the word "personal" is deliberate as Jung also wrote about the "collective unconscious," that repository of humankind's memories, experiences, symbols, rituals, sacred stories, and key events. Joseph L. Henderson defines the collective unconscious as "the part of the psyche which retains and transmits the common psychological inheritance of mankind" (Jung, p.98).

While a wealth of symbolic and mythical material lies in the collective unconscious, so, too, does the *Collective Shadow*. Just as individuals need to name, confront, and incorporate their *Shadows*, so, too, do societies. A prime example of this would be post-apartheid South Africa which, under the leadership of Archbishop Desmond Tutu, brought together the victims and perpetrators of race-based violence to share their stories and give and receive forgiveness. Only then, having confronted its *Shadow*, could the nation move forward.

Jung sometimes used the image of an iceberg to distinguish between consciousness and unconsciousness. The tip of the iceberg lies above the waterline and represents our conscious self — everything of which we are aware or can quickly recall. The mass of the iceberg, however, is hidden under the waterline, out of sight and out of mind, and represents our unconscious self, the home of *The Shadow*.

Definition of the Shadow

According to Jung, each of us goes through life with a *Shadow*, that part of ourselves that has been ignored, repressed, or denied. Over time, this *Shadow* grows, gaining strength from all our unresolved conflicts, resentments, misunderstandings, buried talents, forgotten dreams and desires, unconscious projections, and other liabilities. In fact, the more we deny *The Shadow*, the stronger it becomes, not only manifesting in dreams but also sabotaging our relationships, projects, and the various roles we play. "A man likes to believe he is the master of his soul," writes Jung. "But as long as he is unable to control his moods and emotions, or to be conscious of the myriad secret ways in which unconscious factors insinuate themselves into his arrangements and decisions, he is certainly not his own master" (Jung, p.72). The good news is that when we gradually confront and integrate *The Shadow*, it has the potential to transform us as powerfully as an alchemist could transform base metals into gold!

In his seminal work, *Owning Your Own Shadow*, Robert A. Johnson explains that our *Shadow* is what "we fail to see or know … the refused and unacceptable characteristics [that] collect in the dark corners of our personality" (p.4). In describing what happens when we attempt to see our *Shadow*, Marie-Louise Von Franz explains that we suddenly become aware that the qualities and impulses we find repugnant in others mirror our own deficiencies — "such things as egotism, mental laziness, and sloppiness; unreal fantasies, schemes, and plots; carelessness and cowardice; inordinate love of money and possessions" (Jung, p.174). These dark forces have a habit of tripping us up in life. Warning us that *"Shadow Work"* can be as overwhelming as Hercules' task of cleaning out the dung from the Augean Stables, Von Franz lets us know that *The Shadow* consists of more than omissions. It not only shows up as "impulsive or inadvertent" acts, but before we have time to think, "the evil remark pops out, the plot is hatched, the wrong decision is made, and one is confronted with results that were never intended or consciously wanted" (Jung, p.175).

Coaching Shadow-Driven Clients

I should stress that clients do not go into coaching to address *The Shadow*; however, when *The Shadow* manifests in a coaching engagement or a single coaching session, coaches need to recognize it and respond. Now, *The Shadow* is a master of disguises and generally keeps a low profile during discovery calls, contracting, and first sessions. Gradually, as coaching progresses, *The Shadow* becomes bolder and begins to make its presence felt.

Typically, clients are unaware of their *Shadow* and rather than pointing to their own character flaws, they would rather blame the individuals, groups, and institutions they perceive have wronged them. Often, they project their worst failings and most unsavory character traits onto others, in effect demonizing them. This tendency protects them from ever having to face themselves, for they now have convenient scapegoats to carry their sins out into the wilderness. Conversely, projection can also take the form of hero worship. Robert Johnson points out that it is easier to admire someone from afar than to claim our own capacity for nobility. Either way, whether we project light or darkness, we "do damage to another" by making that person bear our own light or darkness. We also damage ourselves (Johnson, p.46).

Whether or not *The Shadow* can be addressed in coaching depends upon the degree to which it dominates the client. By definition, *Shadow* narratives are filled with litanies about bad luck, betrayals, injustice, bad treatment, missed opportunities, lack of recognition, poor health, and other complaints. These narratives are seldom shared with humor; instead, they are typically replete with anger, resentment, and bitterness. However, as clients become more self-aware, these feelings begin to subside, and they are more willing to accept personal responsibility for all the baggage weighing them down.

In contrast, *Shadow*-driven clients never seem to approach an "Ah-ha" moment. Instead, they constantly repeat key episodes to elicit as much sympathy as they can possibly squeeze out of their coach. Whining and complaining may degenerate into expressions of rage and hatred, character assassinations, and the desire for revenge. When *Shadow* elements are fear-based, then a kind of emotional and moral paralysis sets in; the client is unable to do the "right" thing and resists any process of self-reflection.

When someone is *Shadow*-driven in this way, then *Shadow-work* rightly belongs in a trained Jungian analyst's office. The coach may notice feeling drained after a session with a particular client or troubled by the direction of the coaching conversation. The coach may also begin to dread meeting with this client or sense that little progress is being made. This is where supervision would be a plus!

Questions for Supervision

The first step in supervision would be to assess how working with a *Shadow*-driven client may have a negative impact on various aspects of the coach's life — physically, emotionally, spiritually, and professionally. With input from a trusted guide, the coach can reflect on the following questions:

Do I still have a positive regard for this client?

- Can I respond to this client with compassion?
- Am I hopeful that this client will eventually be able to make progress by working with me?

- Do I have the necessary physical, emotional, and spiritual strength to continue working with this client?
- What price am I paying by continuing to work with this client?
- How much time do I spend thinking about this client in between sessions?
- How is coaching this client having a negative impact on my other coaching relationships?
- How is coaching this client undermining my sense of self and my trust in my coaching abilities?
- What is this client triggering in me?

These and other questions pave the way for taking a hard look at options; these might include:

- Ending coaching and referring the client to therapy.
- Continuing coaching but insisting that the client also work with a therapist.
- Renegotiating the contract to focus on specific goals and desired outcomes.
- Continuing coaching the client in the direction of self-awareness, using regular coaching "tools" such as mirroring and asking powerful questions.

Should the coach decide on Option 4, then ongoing supervision would be essential.

Facilitating Awareness

The International Coaching Federation (ICF) defines Core Competency 7 "Evokes Awareness" in this way: "Facilitates client insight and learning by using tools and techniques such as powerful questioning, silence, metaphor, or analogy." This is no easy task, for to facilitate awareness in another, we must first become aware ourselves, especially when *Shadow*-work is involved. As coaches, we — like other inner guides — are likely to identify with the *Light*, seeing ourselves as bearers of *Light*, promoters of *Light*, icons of *Light*. And many of us are, most of the time. Problems arise when we ignore our *Shadows*, seeing ourselves as the source of *Light*, not as its servant. Helping others "see" and begin to make positive changes can become food for a hungry *Shadow*, especially if we forget our own stories of redemption or if we have never experienced some kind of *"Fall"* in life. I'm using theological terms here because they best communicate the danger of being too "squeaky clean," too perfect, too impressed with our own accomplishments. Robert Johnson writes, "To refuse the dark side of one's nature is to store up or accumulate the darkness"; he goes on to claim that when a society worships its light side and rejects the dark, "this residue appears as wars, economic chaos, strikes, racial intolerance" (26).

The perfect child who grows into the perfect adult often has a monstrous *Shadow* raging within. This can erupt in cruel and destructive ways, often projecting its fury onto the most innocent and vulnerable through verbal, physical, and sexual abuse or passive aggression. Conversely, those who have made mistakes and suffered the consequences are aware of the "Amazing Grace" that saved them from their wretchedness. Unlike their "perfect" counterparts, these *"Wounded Healers"* identify as transmitters of *Light*, not as the Light itself; humbled by all they have gone through, they are content to serve on the sidelines rather than be center stage.

One way we can keep our *Shadow* in check is to perform a regular self-inventory — not an ordinary "examination of conscience" but a *"Shadow Checklist."* Here are some questions and statements that might be helpful:

Shadow Checklist

- Who are some of the specific people whom I dislike or with whom I have had a conflictual relationship?
- What characteristics do I see in them that I find most unpleasant or even repulsive?
- Which of those characteristics might they see in me?
- What does it feel like to acknowledge that I might be more like "them" than I care to admit?
- What groups do I tend to avoid and why?
- What invitations do I tend to refuse and why?
- What types of situations trigger fear, shame, or embarrassment?
- What types of situations leave me feeling insecure or inadequate?
- What types of people do I find intimidating?
- What types of people do I put on a pedestal?
- What is the last thing I would want people to know about me?
- What is the most important thing I want people to know about me?
- Which of my dreams and desires are unfulfilled?
- Which of my dreams and desires have been fulfilled?
- My greatest failure is…
- My greatest success is…
- My greatest fear is…
- My greatest hope is…
- My strongest regret is…
- My happiest childhood memory is…
- My saddest childhood memory is…
- If I could go back in time, I would…
- If I could apologize to anyone, it would be…
- If I could forgive anyone, it would be…

- If I could change anything about my life, it would be...

SUMMARY

- For Carl G. Jung, the personal *Shadow* resides in the personal unconscious.
- The image of an iceberg represents both the conscious self (the tip of the iceberg above the waterline) and the unconscious (everything below the waterline).
- *The Shadow* consists of forgotten dreams, memories, and other repressed material.
- When we gradually confront and integrate *The Shadow*, it can become "gold"!
- When we deny *The Shadow*, it gains strength and can become more destructive.
- *Shadow*-driven clients blame others and reject Truth.
- Coaches working with *Shadow*-driven clients need to be in supervision.

"Between Years"

We like to think that
Midnight splits the years,
Severing old from new
With the cold efficiency
Of a butcher's cleaver.
In our revelry, we proclaim
Misrule's timely end—
The banishing of ill health,
Lucklessness, the blues
And all that threatens
Boisterous abandon.
We drink liberally,
Drowning memories
Of setbacks, stabs, and pricks,
Spilling champagne
As a libation to those gods
We hope to humor.
Sounding noise makers,
Securing paper hats,
We curse enemies,
Bless friends,
Kiss, embrace,
Bang pots and pans
While singing "Auld Lang Syne."
But even as the countdown ends
And church bells peal,
I see the bloody scraps
Of last year's leavings—
Ghosts that will haunt,
Wounds that will fester,

From one hour
To the next...

Woman Dreamer, 1989

CHAPTER TWELVE

Coaching *The Shadow*

Being prepared to coach *The Shadow* doesn't mean that one will get to do so. In fact, when meeting a prospective client for a discovery session or for the first contracted session, I can't imagine that a coach would be thinking, "I wonder how *The Shadow* is going to manifest this time!" For most of us, *The Shadow* is the last thing on our minds as we embark on a coaching journey with a client. Trained to hold clients in "positive regard," we view them not as patients in need of healing (therapeutic model) but as creative partners in a discovery process. Such a journey is very different than accompanying someone in "*Shadow* work," but as mentioned in the previous chapter, *The Shadow* can appear when least expected.

New insight into *The Shadow* emerged from a conversation with my grandson, Vance, whom I had asked to provide some artistic representations of *The Shadow* for use in presentations and workshops. Vance, a first-year college student majoring in art, came up with three design concepts, and I found his charcoal interpretations fascinating. The first illustration captures the resistance of *The Shadow* towards any exposure to the Light. What is hidden wishes to remain hidden where it has lingered undisturbed for months, years, even decades. Its survival as a creature of the dark depends upon its being left in the dark, hence its hostility to any form of exposure. Hand raised in warning, it says, "Go no further! Come no nearer! Probe no deeper!"

When a client's *Shadow* is resistant to change, the coach can feel this physically. Typically, the client is non-cooperative and carries an aura of negativity. Blaming others, making excuses for not following through, and avoiding any form of vulnerability are characteristics of *The Shadow*-possessed client. Coaching sessions will feel like a battleground. Instead of engaging in a free exchange of ideas and a process of exploration, this client will cling to his or her version of the universe. Unwilling to consider new perspectives or suggestions, the client will often answer the coach's questions in monosyllables or else monopolize the session with material from old "tapes." If the coach expresses curiosity, the client changes the subject. Should the coach offer a suggestion, the client shoots it down; and when the coach attempts to mirror back what the client is saying, the response is more or less, "That's not what I meant at all!"

In a worst-case scenario, the client will begin to associate the coach with the "enemy," responding to observations as criticisms, curiosity as snooping, and suggestions as meddling. This type of projection distorts the coach-coachee relationship as the client has now transferred inner chaos and culpability onto the coach. Convinced of his or her innocence, the client feels under attack, even threatened by the coach's clarifying questions. Any attempt at excavating the Truth is met with resistance, even hostility. As for establishing "next steps," this is impossible because nothing has changed, especially the client. Whatever the client indicated would be the desired outcome of the coaching agreement is no closer to being actualized than it was in the contracting stage. Under these circumstances, coaching is impossible and, as suggested in the previous chapter, termination may be the kindest and most ethical response.

Having to terminate a client is not a pleasant experience, even if termination brings relief. In the first place, there is the awkwardness of having to explain to a client why you can no longer work together. Honesty is called for, but it cannot come across as accusing, blaming, or criticizing. On the contrary, whatever the coach has to say must be delivered with respect and compassion — and even then, it is likely to evoke a negative response, whether this be anger towards the coach or increased feelings of self-loathing and worthlessness. Rather than say, "I can't work with you anymore because ...," the coach could invite the client to revisit their initial agreement. Then the conversation might go something like this:

COACH: "We've been working together for a few weeks now, so I thought this would be a good time to review our initial agreement. Would you mind if we take a few minutes before starting today's session?"

CLIENT: "I don't see the point of this, but if you think it's important, go ahead."

COACH: "Thank you. Well, when we first met, you named XXX as your priorities, with XXX as your time frame for accomplishing them. I'm just wondering how close you feel you are to meeting these objectives."

CLIENT: "Hmmm ... I'm not sure anything has changed."

COACH: "That's what I'm sensing. Quite honestly, I'm wondering if coaching is the best option for you right now. It may be that the time is not right, or perhaps some of the issues would be best addressed in therapy, or perhaps another coach would be more aligned with your needs."

CLIENT: "So you're suggesting we stop working together?"

COACH: "Yes. I can't in good conscience continue to meet with you when nothing has changed. What are your thoughts?"

CLIENT: "Well, I certainly don't want to go on wasting my money, and I have no intention of hiring a shrink. What is your refund policy?"

At this point, the coach may want to offer a reasonable refund or simply say that payment remains in place for "services rendered." Whatever the decision, not charging for the final session makes sense, as does releasing the client from all future financial obligations.

The above conversation was difficult, but can you imagine how the coaching relationship would end if the coach were confrontational? Here is a re-write of the previous script:

COACH: "You know, I've been noticing that you're not making any progress, and I think it's time we ended this coaching agreement."

CLIENT: "What do you mean? I've been showing up, haven't I? And haven't I been sharing with you what's happening at my job?"

COACH: "Indeed, you have, but you're angry most of the time and repeat yourself constantly. Also, you never listen to my suggestions, answer my questions, or even acknowledge my attempts to clarify what you are saying. It's just not working."

CLIENT: "I can't believe what you're saying to me or how you're treating me! You're just like my boss — I deserve better than this."

And the session ends on a hostile note, with the client threatening to report the coach for ethics violations. Ouch!

Another way of terminating is to use a personal excuse such as one's health, a full schedule, or conflicting commitments on the day of the client's appointment. Such excuses are less likely to lead to hurt feelings or anger, but they need to be true — lying to a client is hardly modeling a coaching mindset!

The second of Vance's illustrations offers more hope. Here, the client's *Shadow* cradles a tiny flame, representing "the passion for self-actualization burning within" (Grant). Instead of a dark, menacing figure with closed eyes and a hand in the "halt" position, *The Shadow* has a lighter aspect and seems more inwardly focused. This, like the other two images, is "impressionistic," with charcoal lines and smudges being open to interpretation. I see two hands raising up dark *Shadow* material from above *The Shadow*-encased flame, as if to liberate it. It is almost as though *The Shadow* itself is participating in its own liberation, bringing to light that which has nearly been extinguished. Someone suggested that the object the hands are holding resembles a crown of thorns with the beginnings of another face beneath it; looking closely, I see that this could indeed be one way of reading the image. It now reminds me of the face of Christ on the Shroud of Turin, with Christ's beard forming a protective space for the flame. Whatever way one interprets the image suggests that consciousness is possible.

When clients show up for coaching with this flame still burning within, they are open to change and, in fact, actively desire it. Even if, at first, they are unaware of the saboteurs lurking in the unconscious, nevertheless, they want to grow and any resistance is usually brief. Instead of projecting their rage and insecurities onto the coach, they are more likely to reflect on their own shortcomings. As *Shadow* material begins to surface in coaching sessions, they gradually let go of their carefully cultivated public *personas* and instead allow the authentic *Self* to reveal itself. Their willingness to be vulnerable allows the coach to be vulnerable as well — to risk making suggestions and asking questions as appropriate.

Let's imagine that a client is the marketing manager of a large urban catering company. Despite all the five-star reviews he and his team have earned on Yelp, Tripadvisor, and other sites, this client has exceeded the company's budget by over 25% for the last two quarters. Having been issued a first written warning, the client is seeking coaching to help improve his fiscal performance.

> **COACH:** "So, what do you hope to accomplish via coaching?"
> **CLIENT:** "I need to turn things around this quarter, or I expect I'll be on the chopping block."
> **COACH:** "Have you already had any verbal warnings?"
> **CLIENT:** "Yes, several times, so this is serious."
> **COACH:** "And what complaints have you received?"
> **CLIENT:** "That I consistently overspend by including too many extras."
> **COACH:** "25% of extras?"
> **CLIENT:** "Yes, I know it sounds excessive, but that's what it takes to bring in the customers and get those five-star reviews."

COACH: "Hmm. Let me pause here… What I'm hearing you say is that you have exceeded your budget for the last two quarters. What about in previous quarters?"

CLIENT: "I was always within budget, though barely. The big difference is that there were fewer customers and our ratings averaged at four stars."

COACH: "OK, so help me with the math here. You had fewer customers but stayed within budget; you were over budget by 25% when you had more customers. From a purely financial perspective, fewer customers and fewer extras translate into profit, while more customers and more extras translate into loss — major loss. Does this make sense?"

CLIENT: "Financially, perhaps, but we now consistently have five-star ratings."

COACH: "And how important is this to the company?"

CLIENT: "Well, of course, everyone is pleased, and there are five-star reviews all over the website. This makes everyone look good."

COACH: "And how important are the five stars to you?"

CLIENT: (Reflective pause): "Very important."

COACH: "OK?"

CLIENT: "They prove I've accomplished something."

COACH: "I'm listening."

CLIENT: "Yes, I've finally got the recognition I never had at school — or at home. I was always the four-star kid, the B student, the second-best child. You know, it hurts after a while…"

COACH: "And those five stars give you the affirmation you have always wanted and felt you deserved?"

CLIENT: "Yes. I never thought of it that way before, but I think this is what's happening. Every time the team gets a five-star review, I feel it was awarded to me — and the more extras I throw in to sweeten the deal, the more likely I am to get my five stars."

COACH: "I think you're on target here. With your permission, perhaps we can now focus on how you can find intrinsic affirmation for what you do, rather than relying on the ratings of strangers. How does this sound?"

CLIENT: "Sounds like a plan!"

The coaching session ends on a positive note. Though the client's original agenda was to explore how to cut expenses and bring his department within budget, the invisible "saboteur" is his need for recognition. This insight represents his *Epiphany Moment* and the foundation upon which he and his coach can now design next steps. *The Shadow*, of course, lay deep within his unconscious in those painful memories of being "second best." That material is content better suited to therapy.

When clients reach this phase of *Shadow* work, they begin to recognize the triggers that set them off, as well as the origins of those triggers. If some event or association triggers a painful or unpleasant memory, they pause, take a deep breath, and focus on any emotional or physiological shifts that may be taking place. Instead of reacting to the stimuli, they observe what is happening, thus preventing an "emotional hijack." Whereas someone who is *Shadow*-driven is likely to lash out in anger, withdraw, shut down, or become passive-aggressive, the person who is *Shadow*-savvy learns how to prevent undesirable outcomes.

For example, an employee who experienced discrimination as a young child may be rage-filled when a co-worker cracks an offensive joke or makes a comment that is "politically incorrect." Unable to distinguish the joke in poor taste from bullying, the offended employee may punch the joker in the face or pummel the offender mercilessly. In contrast, a more aware person will pause to consider the nature of the offense and the probable outcome of resorting to violence.

The ability to name the triggered emotion, to pause long enough to say, "I am feeling this because..." and to intercept any negative outcome involves seeing patterns. With a coach's encouragement, the client can ask, "When have I been triggered in similar situations, and what were the outcomes?" When the client becomes aware of how certain triggers typically impact his or her thoughts, feelings, and behaviors, transformation happens in every aspect of life, from relationships to the world of work. The task is to become conscious of unconscious forces and "emotionally intelligent."

Emotional Intelligence (EQ) is the ability to recognize and monitor our emotions, to understand their origins and to differentiate between those likely to have positive outcomes and those guaranteed to cause negative outcomes (the "saboteurs"). It keeps us in balance by providing trustworthy information to guide our thinking and behaviors. At the same time, it prevents "emotional hijack" by the amygdala, the primitive brain, and activates the pre-frontal cortex.

Ultimately, the client needs to ask, "How can I change the old patterns to become the owner of my own soul?" The following diagram illustrates the shift that is needed:

- **Old Pattern** = Trigger → activated negative memory → predictable negative response → predictable negative outcome
- **New Pattern** = Trigger → **PAUSE** → awareness of Trigger, understanding of possible outcomes, consideration of choices → averted negative outcome

Vance's third image depicts the integration of *Shadow* and psyche. Long tangled tendrils and swirls remind me of slender branching dendrites arising from neurons and communicating with other neurons. *The Shadow* now seems to dance in a vast sea of connectivity, and the energy is palpable. You can almost feel the image rotating, the spherical head taking in everything, though no eyes are visible. Surprisingly, to the right of the image is a faint embryonic form — or is it angelic? It, too, seems to have dendrites and is connected to *The Shadow* image, which now seems almost maternal. Vance describes this as "the integration of *Shadow* and psyche forming an armor of understanding that protects the mind from leading it astray" (Grant).

When clients in the process of integrating *The Shadow* show up for coaching, the possibilities are endless. They bring with them energy, enthusiasm, and the determination to make progress. They are curious and inspire curiosity; they welcome suggestions and insights; they pause to reflect and are comfortable with silence. Such clients understand they are in a "discovery process" and are willing to let revelation lead in its own time and in its own way. Far from considering themselves victims, they see themselves as the authors of their own narratives, taking responsibility when appropriate while forgiving those who may have caused them injury. They are humble and grateful, compassionate and wise. Though they may have suffered much, they are at peace and feel called to serve others. For them, life is full of wonder and mystery; their greatest passion is to be fully alive.

How wonderful to have such clients! They are living proof of the alchemy through which the base substance of *The Shadow* can be spun into gold. To work with them is to dive into the depths and to surface renewed and refreshed, to become not just a work in progress but a new creation. It is a journey of transformation for both coach and client, and any *Epiphanies* offer shared experiences of the sacred. Whether clients are at the stage of recognizing *The Shadow* or integrating it, dreamwork can be a useful coaching tool. Now, I'm not suggesting deep dream analysis or anything that rightfully belongs in therapy, but what can safely be described as the "coach approach" to dreamwork. In most cases, this will occur with individuals, not teams, and will be initiated by the client. In other words, the coach won't begin a session by randomly asking, "Have you had any *Shadow* dreams recently?" but will know how to respond when a client volunteers, "I've had some disturbing dreams recently that I would like to share with you."

Of course, some coaches may not be comfortable exploring their clients' dream lives, but one doesn't have to be a certified dream analyst to help them understand what their dreams might be trying to communicate. The most important task is to listen to the details and note any vivid imagery, emotionally charged words, and the relevance of the dream narrative to a situation the client may be experiencing in waking life.

In *Shadow* dreams, there is usually a menacing presence of some kind that poses a threat to the dreamer. In some cases, the presence may be human and may even resemble someone known to the dreamer; in others, the figure could be a wild animal, an alien from outer space, or even an inanimate object that threatens to devour the dreamer. In addition, *The Shadow* can manifest in plural form — as a mob, a battalion of enemy forces, a swarm of killer bees, or a squadron of rogue drones. Typically, *Shadow* dreams leave dreamers feeling shaken, even terrified; they may have a sense of impending disaster or may be convinced that they — or someone close to them — is facing calamity, even death. They often awaken feeling exhausted and disturbed.

So, how is the coach to proceed? The good news is that it is always the dreamer who is best qualified to decipher the dream. The language of dreams may seem like some exotic code, but the symbols are generally ones that the dreamer can interpret — with a little help. Dream material may sometimes include data from the collective unconscious, but most dreams emerge from the dreamer's personal unconscious — that depository of forgotten or repressed personal experiences, dreams, and desires. Only the dreamer can fully understand this material, so the task of the coach is really nothing more than to ask the right questions.

If the client asks permission to share a dream, the coach might, in turn, ask if they can adjust the coaching agenda for that day. That way, both coach and client are clear that the dream will be the priority, perhaps at the expense of their contracted agreed-upon focus. The coach may also want to remind the client that any therapeutic work with dreams belongs in therapy and that the coach's approach will be to explore what the dream might reveal in terms of coaching issues.

When working with dreams, I generally begin by inviting the client to share the dream, whether it consists of a mere fragment or a lengthy narrative. I take notes, record anything that strikes me, and ask clarifying questions, especially if some element of the dream is confusing. Then I have a list of questions I can draw on, as needed. I don't necessarily ask all these questions, but just the ones that seem helpful:

1. **What is your dream's title?** When given spontaneously, the answer to this question can reflect the dream's thematic content.
2. **What emotion did you feel on waking up?** This question can also help us understand the dream's message. While there may be terrifying events in the dream, the dreamer may awaken feeling peaceful, even happy; conversely, the dreamer may have dreamt of spring flowers on a sunny day but awakened feeling dread.
3. **What images in the dream stand out to you and why?** In dreams with multiple images, it is helpful to separate the "major" symbols from the less important ones. Jungians believe that everything within a dream represents some aspect of the dreamer, but given the time limitation of a coaching session, it is sometimes impossible to explore the client's associations with every symbol. However, this is an activity that the client may wish to pursue outside the session as there is nothing extraneous in a dream.
4. **Were you in the dream or observing the action?** Sometimes, the dreamer is right in the heart of the action, and sometimes, the action takes place while the dreamer observes events as if they were in a movie.

5. **Which character were you in the dream, and how do you know it was you?** This is always a fascinating question. There are times when the dreamer looks exactly like himself or herself in the dream, and times when the dreamer looks like someone else or even appears as an animal or supernatural being of some kind — a magician, a witch, a saint, a guru… However, some tell-tale quality lets the dreamer know that he is the ogre or that she is the damsel in distress!
6. **Who is The Shadow in the dream?** This is where we get to the heart of the matter. What image or images are threatening the dreamer and why? What does this *Shadow* look like? How is it interacting with the dreamer and the rest of the cast of characters? What makes this figure threatening?
7. **What would happen if you could confront The Shadow?** This is a crucial point in dreamwork. If the dreamer can re-enter the dream and, instead of fleeing, turn around and ask *The Shadow* directly, "What do you want of me?" amazing revelations may surface. *The Shadow* is usually some aspect of the dreamer working against the dreamer's best interests, e.g. that part of the dreamer that is sabotaging self-advancement or integration.
8. **What is the theme of your dream?** This question entails looking at the information that has surfaced thus far and reflecting on general meaning. Themes might include refusing to delegate, taking too many risks, refusing to adapt to changing times, becoming too attached to something or someone, neglecting a relationship, etc.
9. **What does this dream want of you?** Here, the coach and client can explore the "next steps." The dream has brought some new awareness, and, as a result, the dreamer has some obligation to fulfill. This may involve contacting an old friend, giving an employee a second chance, applying

for a promotion, declining a stressful invitation, avoiding taking some risk, or slowing down while driving.

There are other ways of conducting dreamwork, including in group settings, but in a one-on-one coaching session, these questions can help the dreamer reflect on his or her nocturnal experience and de-code the symbolic language, safely and briefly, without diving into the unconscious. Here is an example of how a session might be conducted:

> **CLIENT:** "Would you mind if we worked on a dream today? It seems to be related to some of the other issues we've been discussing."
> **COACH:** "It's your time — where do you want to begin?"
> **CLIENT:** "It's just a fragment, really, but I woke up feeling anxious and unsettled. I'm conscious of running down a grassy path that's emerald green. There are no people, no trees — I can't even see myself, but I know I'm the one running. I'm running fast, as if someone is chasing me, but all I can see is the path. The path is a steep hill and the further down I go, the darker the grass becomes. Suddenly, I find myself in a dark wood and I have no idea where I am. I try looking for my cell phone flashlight, but it won't turn on. I slow down, but I'm now in the heart of darkness and I'm afraid. Something tells me that to find the light again, I must retrace my steps and that going forward is hazardous. So, I turn around and head back, up the hill. Now my cell phone flashlight is working again."
> **COACH:** "Wow. There seems to be a clear message here! What do you think it is?"
> **CLIENT:** "Well, it seems to be warning me that I'm heading towards a danger zone and that the only safety is to retrace my steps."

COACH: "That's the message I'm getting, too. I'm curious as to why you're running or what you're running from."

CLIENT: "I'm not sure but whatever is chasing me is quite close, but I don't see it or feel its presence when I retrace my steps."

COACH: "So when you turn around, it's no longer there?"

CLIENT: "No. I mean, it's not there."

COACH: "I see. And what about the danger zone ahead? Any ideas about that?"

CLIENT: "It seems that whatever is chasing me will catch me if I continue into the darkness and that the only way I can be safe is to turn around."

COACH: "Is there anything chasing you in your waking life? You said the dream could be related to issues we have already discussed."

CLIENT: "What's coming to mind are all those project deadlines and all the new work that the leadership team is piling on me."

COACH: "What might happen if you continue accepting new projects while you struggle to meet deadlines?"

CLIENT: "I could be facing a breakdown or major health problem. I see it now — my workload is unsustainable…"

COACH: "So the dream is warning you to stop and return to a healthier balance?"

CLIENT: "Yes — I have to stop doing everyone else's work and learn to say 'No' to my supervisor."

COACH: "It sounds like you already know your next steps!"

CLIENT: "You bet! This has been very helpful!"

This whole exchange lasts no more than 10–15 minutes and only involves a few of the questions I listed earlier. Brief as it is, however, dreamwork allows the client to see the impact of a stressful work situation and the need to achieve more life balance. The greatest insight, perhaps, is that continuing the present path could bring catastrophic health outcomes. The coach's ability to stay with the client allows the client to reach potentially life-saving conclusions.

The "Jeremy Taylor" Approach

There is a simpler approach to dreamwork that is highly effective both with individual clients and with groups. This is the "Jeremy Taylor" approach, which I learned from friend and colleague Peter Metzner, who was fortunate enough to have studied with the late Rev Taylor. The method reinforces the reality that the dreamer is always the best interpreter of the dream, removing any expectation that the coach is "the expert." Taylor, a dreamworker, author, and Unitarian Universalist minister, would facilitate dream groups in the following way:

1. The dreamer narrates the dream in its entirety.
2. Members of the dream group ask clarifying questions.
3. Having listened to the clarifying answers, one by one, group members offer the following response, *"If this were my dream..."* (Here add appropriate tags, e.g. "If this were my dream, I would wonder..."; "If this were my dream, I would be curious..."; "If this were my dream, I would be concerned...").
4. The dreamer then thanks the group for their input and shares which comments have brought the most insights and why.

Peter and I have used this approach to dreamwork in a course we co-teach at The Institute for Life Coach Training, "Coaching through Story." I have witnessed firsthand the amazing breakthroughs students have experienced just by listening to their classmates say, "If this were my dream..." It is a brief, nonjudgmental process that any coach can use, whether a fan of Carl Jung or not and whether trained in dreamwork or not.

SUMMARY

- When *The Shadow* resists change, the coach can feel this physically; coaching soon becomes a battleground.
- A client fully in the grip of *The Shadow* is usually uncoachable.
- Terminating a client, if necessary, must be done with respect and compassion.
- Even if hidden saboteurs lurk in the unconscious, a client's desire for growth makes coaching possible and desirable.
- A *Shadow*-driven client responds instinctually to negative triggers; in contrast, a *Shadow*-savvy client pauses to reflect on the trigger's origins and the possible negative outcomes that might occur by reacting to it.
- When the client is self-actualized and does authentic *Shadow* work, this creates the optimum coaching relationship.
- Dreamwork is a powerful tool for both encountering and integrating *The Shadow*.
- There are many ways of utilizing dreamwork in coaching. This chapter provides my approach, based loosely on Jungian concepts, as well as the Jeremy Taylor approach.

"Misbegotten"

The men who made the myth
Murdered woman,
Molding proverbial rib
Not in the divine image
But into a veritable Lilith
Whose lascivious ways
Unleashed sin
And ensured thralldom
For all her daughters.

***

They clothed her
In iridescence,
Endowed her with the charm
Of a devil's gateway,
And she, Adam's helpmate,
Unsealed the forbidden tree
With serpent's guile.

***

We who have broken free
From fig leaves, succulent fruit
And patriarchal bondage
Wonder at this midwifery
Which first gave evil
Female form

And see in Eve's birthing
The throes of our kind.

***

Extraordinary Time, 1988

CHAPTER THIRTEEN

Archetypal Awareness

Are you a *Magician,* a *Wanderer,* a *Warrior,* a *Lover,* or a *Fool*? Or perhaps you're a *Sage,* an *Artist,* a *Hero,* or a *Savior*? Or an *Orphan,* a *Teacher,* a *Healer,* or a *Leader*? Or a *Rebel,* a *Student,* a *Liberator,* or a *Tyrant*? Or perhaps you are all of these or none of these realities. Or perhaps you are an *Orphan* at home, a *Leader* at work, a *Mystic* in your faith community, a *Prophet* in your political community and a *Child* when you're out with your friends. Then again, you might be a great *Leader* in one area of life and a bad *Leader* in another — a kind of Jekyll and Hyde. Gandhi, for example, was an enlightened *Leader* at a national and global level, but some say he dominated his wife in his personal life. Mother Teresa of Calcutta is internationally hailed as a saint, but some who knew her say she withheld aid from the dying because she believed it was good for them to suffer. Both were saints and tyrants — the same archetype but different manifestations.

Whether conscious of this or not, we are driven or guided by inner forces or "archetypes" — that is, by universal patterns of behavior that occur in the world's myths, historical narratives, and literature. This means that regardless of the culture or the era in which they appear, these recognizable patterns share many features in common. Take *The Hero,* for example. If we place Beowulf, Luke Skywalker, Harry Potter, Wonder Woman, Odysseus, Harriet Tubman, Dr Martin Luther King, Jr, Mother Teresa, Mahatma Gandhi, Cesar Chavez, Katherine Johnson, Malala Yousafzai, and Nelson Mandela side by side, we may at first be unable to note any similarities. In fact, the very diversity of this assortment of mythical figures, big-screen characters, and historical luminaries is baffling. Luke Skywalker and Mother Teresa? Harry Potter and Katherine Johnson?

A closer look, however, will reveal that these fictional and historical characters defied all odds for the sake of a cause, an ideal, a project, or a group of people, pushing beyond limits and "sacrificing" themselves or their best interests in the process. While Mother Teresa tended to the poor and dying on the streets of Calcutta, Luke Skywalker embarked on a harrowing rescue mission to find Princess Leia and battle the Galactic Empire. And while Harry Potter used his wizardry to protect his friends and undermine evil forces, Katherine Johnson broke boundaries of race and gender to provide the mathematical calculations upon which NASA based its first crewed space flights.

To be a *Hero*, then, demands courage, conviction, altruism, and steadfastness; it involves speaking Truth, seeking the good, and pouring oneself out for the sake of humanity. I would add that *Heroes* typically rely on "inner power" rather than external force. They diffuse violent situations not with weapons but with the power of their words and actions. They defy structures of oppression through civil disobedience, passive resistance, and creative strategies for bypassing limiting rules and regulations. They don't accept "No" for an answer but insist on pursuing the impossible until it becomes a possibility. They not only have a dream but also believe in it and empower others to believe in it as well! Greater than life, they spend their lives for the sake of others, often losing their lives in the process.

Other familiar archetypal patterns include *The Holy Child, The Leader, The Teacher, The Savior, The Warrior, The Adventurer, The Lover, The Caregiver, The Inventor,* and *The Magician,* but the list is inexhaustible. As in the case of *The Hero* archetype, there are global exemplars for each category. When I think of *The Holy Child*, for example, I not only visualize the child Jesus but also Moses in the bulrushes, Romulus and Remus, baby Krishna, and the infant Buddha. What also comes to mind is the time of innocence that Dylan Thomas captures in his poem *Fern Hill* and that William Wordsworth evokes in *Ode on Intimations of Immortality*. For Thomas, for example, the world of his boyhood was green and golden, happy and singing, and in those "lamb white days" when he was prince of the apple towns, huntsman and herdsman, he was oblivious that Time held him "green and dying." Like Wordsworth's growing boy, "shades of the prison house" began to close in on him — as they do on all of us — as he began to forget the "glory and the dream."

Images of *Heroes, Saviors, Tricksters, Teachers, Artists, Fools, Warriors, Caregivers, Lovers,* and *Magicians* not only populate the world of literature and art but also our imaginations. When archetypes are in balance, they function as guides, helping us become our best selves. We have seen that *The Hero* teaches us to persist, struggle, and overcome, even when life presents overwhelming challenges. *The Sage* offers clarity and perspective when we have lost our way, while *The Magician* can help us transform the forces of chaos or subdue Evil. *The Healer* has a special gift of empathy, which can be a source of comfort to those in physical or emotional pain. *Teachers* have a wealth of information to share, often giving generously their wisdom and resources.

However, when one archetype is dominant, it can become tyrannical, even destructive, to ourselves and others. *The Beautiful Queen* can become *The Wicked Witch; The Benign Ruler* may morph into *The Ogre Tyrant; The Magician* sometimes degenerates into *The Wicked Sorcerer*. Each archetype has its own energy, but this can have both a positive and negative aspect. For better or worse, they are guiding forces, either bringing out the best in us or leading us into grandiosity, cruelty, and other regrettable character defects. Both Gandhi and Hitler, for example, were gripped by *The Leader* archetype. While Gandhi was inspired to use "soul power" to oppose British oppression in India, the same archetype propelled Hitler into genocide and the push for global domination. Identifying with *The Leader* made a saint of one man and a devil of the other.

In Life Coaching and other forms of inner guidance, archetypes show up with regularity. Sometimes, the archetypes that surface create bridges into a new future. Clients may see themselves as *Wanderers* about to embark on a voyage into the unknown, or as *Heroes* defeating monstrous dragons, or as *Magicians* who can transform a non-descript life into a spectacular, passion-filled adventure. At other times the archetypes may reveal sinister forces — addictions, soul-destroying relationships, emotional baggage that has yet to be dealt with, self-doubts, fears, bad habits, and dangerous inclinations. These may surface as *Evil Emperors, Wicked Witches, Vampires, Tyrants, Sorcerers, Assassins,* and other manifestations of *The Shadow*. By recognizing such archetypes, the client can confront abusers, chastise oppressors, banish toxic people, disempower bullies, and, most importantly, re-affirm or claim personal power. Identifying the archetypes driving our clients can help us de-code whether they are trustworthy guides or out-of-control tyrants, whether they are life-giving or death-dealing. The archetypes that manifest in clients' narratives reveal much about their values, hopes, fears, and challenges. Their images help us understand dimensions of their experience that would otherwise be inaccessible. Powerful questions surface, and these, in turn, lead to profound discoveries and more heightened awareness. From this vantage point, we can help our clients discern how to find balance by cultivating new archetypes; together, we can explore ways in which some archetypes may become more active while others may lessen their grip. For each client, the journey will be different but the goal of achieving a healthier, happier *Self* will be the desired outcome for everyone!

Coaches attuned to the mythical imagination are well-equipped to draw on archetypes in their work of facilitating awareness. In *Mind-Shifting Imagery*, I note:

"The coach well-versed in myths, archetypes, and biblical stories is at an advantage here. Images of 'flying too high' might trigger memories of the Icarus story; an ordinary citizen heroically taking on a corporate giant might remind us of David and Goliath; somebody who faces multiple tasks might be living the story of *The Labors of Hercules;* the client who is pushing hard and getting nowhere may be a modern-day Sisyphus…" (Stewart, p.23).

The starting point, however, is always to be *self-aware* — and this means understanding our own active archetypes! Since there are infinite archetypes, focusing on those that typically drive anyone involved in offering inner guidance may be useful. First on the list — especially for new coaches — is *The Rescuer*. While this archetype, like *The Hero*, is courageous, self-sacrificing, and determined to see the mission through, it can take over a coaching session, disempowering the client while inflating the coach's ego. *Rescuers* have their place: they run into burning buildings and dive into murky waters to haul out the living and those who are barely alive; if they linger too long, however, they create dependency. Instead of growing, the "rescued" see themselves as "survivors" or, worse still, as victims. Coaches need to remember that clients are whole as they are and that they can transcend their limiting situations, with or without the coach. The trap for coaches is wanting to be needed or feeling that they know what is best for the client!

Another archetype that can grip the coach is that of *The Teacher,* especially for those of us with educational backgrounds. Now, there are occasions when briefly sharing useful information may benefit the client, but when the coach moves from listening to teaching, losing the client's agenda in the process, there is clearly a problem. The coach's task is not to provide information but to collaborate with the client in a discovery process. The client already has the knowledge base needed to move forward but often requires encouragement and guidance. The coach's responsibility is facilitating the client's awareness, not providing answers!

Yet another archetype to hold at bay, especially for therapists and former therapists, is that of *The Healer*. Now, all coaching involves healing of some kind, whether healing a sense of failure, lack of courage, inability to make decisions, or reluctance to delegate. Still, when the coach leads the clients down the rabbit hole into past traumas or precipitating events, then coaching ceases to be coaching and becomes therapy instead. Just because the coach has therapeutic tools that might benefit the client, there is no reason to use them; in fact, to do so violates the *International Coaching Federation's Code of Ethics* and most likely upturns the coaching agreement.

At the end of this chapter, you will find several resources to help you identify and regulate the archetypes driving you personally and professionally. The first is a list of common archetypes, followed by questions for reflection. Then comes a simple quiz to help you see how you typically "show up" in team settings. After this, the "De-Coding Archetypes Quiz" focuses on twelve archetypes that often surface in inner guidance or coaching. Please note that these tools are not scientifically based and are intended for personal reflection only. I do not recommend sharing them with clients directly; rather, what you learn from these exercises should heighten your intuition and help you respond to the archetypes that may surface in your coaching sessions.

List of Common Archetypes

Here are just some of the archetypes that surface in myths, dreams, movies, literature, and daily life. You may want to go through this list and note which ones have driven you in the past and which ones are active in your life right now. As you look at the list, see if there are any archetypes you would like to banish or whether there are some that you would like to be more active. Feel free to add any missing archetypes to the list!

Achiever, Actor, Adventurer, Angel, Anima, Animus, Apprentice, Artist, Assassin, Athlete, Avenger, Beggar, Betrayer, Braggart, Bully, Caregiver, Challenger, Child, Commander, Companion, Contemplative, Creator, Crone, Dancer, Daredevil, Destroyer, Devil, Dictator, Disciple, Dreamer, Entertainer, Explorer, Father, Femme Fatale, Fool, Gardener, Giver, Glutton, Goddess, Guardian, Guide, Guru, Healer, Hedonist, Helper, Hermit, Hero, Holy Child, Hunter, Individualist, Innocent, Insider, Inventor, Jester, Judge, Juggler, King, Killer, Knight, Leader, Liberator, Lover, Madman, Magician, Maiden, Martyr, Mediator, Mentor, Messenger, Miser, Monk, Mother, Musician, Mystic, Nomad, Nun, Nurturer, Orphan, Outsider, Perfectionist, Persona, Poet, Politician, Priest, Prince, Princess, Prophet, Prostitute, Protector, Queen, Rebel, Reformer, Rescuer, Risk-taker, Romantic, Ruler, Sage, Saint, Savior, Scapegoat, Scholar, Seducer, Seer, Seeker, Self, Senex, Servant, Shadow, Shaman, Shape Shifter, Sinner, Slave, Soldier, Storyteller, Student, Survivor, Teacher, Temptress, Thief, Trickster, Tyrant, Victim, Virgin, Visionary, Wanderer, Warrior, Witch, Wizard, Wounded Healer.

Open-Ended Questions for Reflection

These questions are designed to help you name and evaluate the archetypes currently driving your life. You may want to discuss your results with another coach or else keep a journal to record your responses. The more fully you answer, the more archetypally aware you will become!

1. Which **ten** archetypes currently have the most relevance in your life?

2. Of these ten archetypes, which **three** do you live with each day?
3. Which **one** of these **three** archetypes guides or drives you with the greatest energy?
4. In what ways does this dominant archetype manifest in your life? Give examples.
5. Is your dominant archetype life-giving, death-dealing, or a mixture of the two?
6. What are the positive aspects of your dominant archetype, and what are its negative aspects? Create two columns to list the main ways your archetype "shows up."
7. Are you happy with your dominant archetype, or does it have characteristics you would like to change?
8. How does this archetype manifest in your work as a life coach?
9. What other archetypes already active in your life might balance out *The Shadow* dimensions of your dominant archetype?
10. What other archetypes might you want to invite into your life? How might you "cultivate" them?
11. What archetypes hold you back, and what archetypes guide the future you wish to live?
12. What is your primary image of yourself?
13. How can you dream a new world into being?
14. What is the change you need to embrace?
15. How can you tame dragons without fleeing from them, slaying them, or enabling them?
16. How can you repaint the world, and what colors would you choose?

Team Archetypes

A great team depends on great members and having a variety of personalities on board. Each of the archetypes below has its strengths and weaknesses. Add up the statements you agree with for each type of leader and see which archetype is dominant. There are no right or wrong answers. Be aware that a team of Executive Coaches will be less successful than a team comprised of representatives from every category of team members, including Support Staff and Free Spirits. I have used this simple quiz to form teams and consistently found that the more diverse the team, the more innovative and successful it proves to be. In terms of your team profile and personal growth, consider how your dominant archetype might need to be balanced with another archetype. For example, if you scored the highest for "Executive Coach," cultivating the empathy of the "Team Builder," the creativity of the "Free Spirit," and the service mindset of the "Support Staff" would give you the balance needed for inspired leadership!

The Fearless Leader

1. I am a strategic thinker and can design successful outcomes.
2. I enjoy every challenge and am committed to achieving the best possible outcomes.
3. I never let personal problems interfere with the goals I set for myself.
4. I don't adapt my attitudes or actions to fit others' expectations.
5. I don't get distracted easily.
6. I don't need to be "liked" in the workplace.
7. Others look to me to get things done.
8. I expect my direct reports to work as hard as I do.
9. I have no tolerance for mediocrity.
10. I don't share my personal life with my colleagues.

Score _____

The Executive Coach

1. I don't make decisions based on emotion.

2. I pride myself on my objectivity.
3. I enjoy asking questions that startle listeners into new ways of thinking.
4. I thrive on seeing my clients grow at their own pace.
5. I pay attention to my clients' use of language.
6. I am not as interested in theories as in evidence.
7. People come to me to gain clarity, not consolation.
8. People look to me when they want to set goals.
9. I am skilled at helping others hold themselves accountable.
10. I enjoy helping people design the lives they wish to live.

Score _____

The Consultant on Flextime

1. I prefer to stay in a quiet corner at a party than socialize.
2. No one solves my problems as well as I can do by myself.
3. My mind is more active when I'm alone.
4. I love organizing my home/workspace so everything is in place.
5. During meetings, I prefer to listen to what everyone else says rather than share my ideas.
6. I love quiet activities such as reading, playing with my cat, and handicrafts.
7. I am most productive when I'm working at home.
8. Staff meetings leave me exhausted.
9. Some people assume I'm anti-social, but the reality is that I'm an introvert.
10. Others look to me when they need to reflect on their lives.

Score _____

The Team Builder

1. I love bringing positive energy to the team.
2. I'm skilled at group facilitating and go out of my way to ensure everyone's voice is heard.
3. I try to stay out of office politics.
4. I am the team member who remembers birthdays and anniversaries and who checks in with co-workers when they are ill.
5. I enjoy mentoring new employees.
6. I am the designated driver when I go out with my friends.
7. I place other people's needs before my own.
8. Whenever there is a conflict, I am the one who tries to resolve matters.
9. Others look to me when they need comfort or empathy.
10. I am a good listener and always make time for those who confide in me.

Score _____

The Support Staff

1. If I work on a project and the plans change, I will follow whatever management decides.
2. I am crushed if I contribute to a project but don't receive recognition for my work.
3. If another person mistreats a colleague, I will let them work out their differences rather than intervene.
4. I tend to see the good in everyone.
5. I agree with what others say to avoid conflict.
6. Because of my good nature, others often take advantage of me.
7. Others look to me to help them complete projects.

8. I would rather follow instructions than be responsible for designing actions.
9. When it comes to promotions, I am often "passed over."
10. I tend to be quiet at meetings as I don't have much to contribute.

Score _____

The Free Spirit

1. I am the life of the office and love entertaining my co-workers.
2. I am very open about my private life and enjoy sharing details at work.
3. I find it difficult to maintain long-term relationships.
4. I tend to miss deadlines and can be easily distracted.
5. When it comes to love interests, I get bored easily.
6. I'm highly creative and have endless ideas.
7. I have a hard time following through with my commitments.
8. I am happiest with a flexible schedule that allows me to finish things in my own time.
9. Others look to me when they want creative input or need to be saved from boredom.
10. I dress for impact and am proud of my personal style.

Score _____

Highest Score _____
Second Highest Score _____

Other archetypes that may appear in Teams include: *Ruler, Creator, Visionary, Sage, Explorer, Traditionalist, Warrior, Healer,*

Risk-Taker, Artist, Scientist, Judge, Teacher, Student, Rescuer, Mediator, and *Liberator.*

Twelve Archetypes for Coaches and Other Inner Guides

For better or worse, these twelve archetypes often appear in coaching sessions and in other forms of inner guidance. They are especially relevant for spiritual coaching and spiritual direction, hence the "God language." If you are uncomfortable with the word "God," then feel free to substitute this with any term that evokes a sense of higher consciousness or connection to the spiritual universe.

Some archetypes require a low score, while others work best with a high score. In addition, another archetype can bring a potentially negative archetype into balance. All this might seem very complicated, but once you have taken the quiz, add up the statements you agree with for each archetype, entering them under each archetype's score; then proceed to **Decoding Your Twelve Archetypes. This should help you understand your results!** *Again, this quiz is not meant as a scientific tool but as an opportunity for personal reflection.*

I.   The Teacher Archetype

1. I gain energy from sharing my knowledge with clients.
2. My greatest satisfaction is seeing clients grow.
3. I often provide my clients with helpful resources.
4. I am at my best when explaining new ideas or concepts.
5. I am happiest in the world of ideas and love exploring these topics with anyone who will listen.
6. I often put on my "teacher's hat" while working with a client.
7. My client and I share equal "speaking time."
8. I sometimes find myself correcting a client who may have been mistaken about some fact or situation.

9. People often compliment me on my ability to simplify complex ideas.

   SCORE _____

II. The Healer Archetype

1. I am quick to observe when a client is suffering in any way.
2. I usually know what to suggest when someone is hurting.
3. I understand the connection between physical illness and emotional distress.
4. I feel my client's pain.
5. I can offer comfort to those in distress.
6. People seek me out as a healer.
7. I have suffered in my own life and therefore understand the suffering of others.
8. I receive energy when working with someone who needs healing.
9. I have a calming effect on people who are angry or upset.

   SCORE _____

III. The Sage Archetype

1. I see things clearly, even in complex situations.
2. I always look at both sides of a conflict.
3. I form my opinions when I know the facts.
4. Much of my wisdom comes from life experience.
5. From every disaster, there is a lesson to be learned.
6. I avoid gossip and hearsay.
7. Younger, less experienced people seek me out as a guide or mentor.

8. I don't engage in drama or arguments.
9. People come to see me when they need advice.

SCORE _____

IV. The Savior Archetype

1. I feel compelled to rescue people.
2. I place the needs of others before my own.
3. People come to me because they know I will help them.
4. I will look at every possible solution if someone is in need.
5. I risk my own interests and safety for the sake of others.
6. Sometimes, I offer so much help that others can no longer help themselves.
7. When people ask for help, I give without evaluating if they really need it.
8. Scammers tend to take advantage of me.
9. I derive energy from helping people in distress.

SCORE _____

V. The Dreamer Archetype

1. I believe there is a better world ahead.
2. My goal is to help clients dream of a new future.
3. I believe that all things are possible.
4. Nothing can stop me if I set my mind on something.
5. I feel sad when my clients settle for a world of limitations.
6. I constantly imagine new possibilities.
7. A nightmare, for me, is the inability to dream.
8. Clients come to me when they tire of the old reality.
9. I never cease dreaming.

SCORE _____

VI. The Listener Archetype

1. Clients come to me because I am a good listener.
2. I am skilled at hearing what is not being said.
3. I am silent 95% of the time in a coaching session.
4. I listen with my whole being, not just my ears.
5. I read body language and pay attention to tone of voice.
6. I seldom interrupt a client.
7. I listen to the voice within me and trust what it says.
8. I pay attention to a client's word choices and use of imagery.
9. I listen to the silence, not just to the words.

SCORE _____

VII. The Mystic Archetype

1. I value contemplative time over action.
2. I work best with clients focused on their relationship with God.
3. Clients come to me because they sense my close relationship with God.
4. I lose energy when clients are more concerned with material goals than spiritual growth.
5. I am energized by clients who want to grow in intimacy with God.
6. My need for quiet is as strong as my need to breathe.
7. I avoid seeing clients "back-to-back" as I need to "recharge" between sessions.
8. Prayer and quiet are the foundations of my coaching practice.
9. I rely on the Spirit to guide me when I work with clients.

SCORE _____

VIII. The Judge Archetype

1. I have a clear sense of right and wrong.
2. I hold myself to the highest ethical standards.
3. I hold my clients to the highest ethical standards.
4. I quickly point out the consequences when my clients make bad choices.
5. I can become impatient when my clients repeat the same mistakes over and over.
6. When clients bring misfortune upon themselves, I help them see where they went wrong.
7. I always urge my clients to make amends to those they have harmed.
8. People value my guidance when they want a "new beginning."
9. I can be judgmental at times.

SCORE _____

IX. The Shaman Archetype

1. I am highly intuitive.
2. Having transcended my own brokenness, I help my clients become whole.
3. I understand psychological blocks and patterns.
4. Clients come to me when they feel disconnected from their deepest selves.
5. I thrive on doing "deep soul work" with my clients.
6. I help clients re-discover their soul energy.
7. *Shadow* work allows my clients to embrace the *Light*.
8. I help my clients achieve balance in their lives.
9. I help my clients reconnect with their social circles.

SCORE _____

X. The Prophet Archetype

1. I try to see life from God's perspective.
2. I observe society and often critique what I see.
3. I have a solid commitment to social justice.
4. Clients come to me when they want to change the world.
5. I reassure clients of God's unconditional love for them.
6. I often see life from the perspective of the "underdog."
7. I feel both God's pain and humanity's pain.
8. I speak out boldly, regardless of the consequences.
9. I encourage my clients to find their voice.

SCORE _____

XI. The Guide Archetype

1. I am a great motivator.
2. I work with clients when they are lost "in the dark wood."
3. Clients come to me to work on discernment issues.
4. I have a clear sense of where various paths might lead.
5. I encourage clients to look within for their answers.
6. I point out the danger zones when I see them.
7. I encourage clients to choose what is life-giving.
8. I point out what might be death-dealing.
9. I see life as a spiral to be explored, not as a timeline to be endured.

SCORE _____

XII. The Companion Archetype

1. I see my clients as friends.
2. Clients look to me for support and acceptance.

3. I often share personal stories to help my clients in their journey.
4. I offer food or beverages to my clients when we meet in person.
5. My clients often bring me gifts.
6. I often go "overtime" with my clients.
7. I tend to have "long-term" clients who are very loyal.
8. My clients often contact me by phone or email between sessions.
9. I often find myself wondering how my clients are doing.

SCORE _____

Decoding Your Twelve Archetypes

*First, add up your scores for each archetype and record them in the list that follows. Which archetypes are dominant? Which of these dominant archetypes holds the most energy for you? Which archetypes "tie"? Which archetypes score the lowest? Which archetypes do you intuitively feel **most** reflect your style and presence as a coach or inner guide? Which archetypes do you intuitively feel **least** reflect your style and presence as a coach or inner guide?*

The Teacher _____
The Healer _____
The Sage _____
The Savior _____
The Dreamer _____
The Listener _____
The Mystic _____
The Judge _____
The Shaman _____

The Prophet _____
The Guide _____
The Companion _____

Now review the characteristics of each archetype:

1. **The Teacher:** *The Teacher* has a wealth of information to share and often gives generously of his/her wisdom and resources. On occasion, this can be a real gift to the client; however, when the *Teacher* archetype dominates, then the coach becomes a *Mentor/Teacher*, and the session ceases to be coaching. **To be in balance, *The Teacher* needs to cultivate *The Listener*.**
2. **The Healer:** *The Healer* has a special gift of empathy, which can comfort those in physical or emotional pain. However, when *The Healer* archetype dominates, the coach may lose perspective and listen only to the client's version of events. A high score is desirable for this archetype. **To be in balance, *The Healer* needs to cultivate *The Judge*.**
3. **The Sage:** *The Sage* has gifts of wisdom, clarity, and impartiality. These qualities are especially helpful to those in situations of discernment; however, when *The Sage* archetype dominates, the client may feel "unheard" and "misunderstood." **To be in balance, *The Sage* needs to cultivate *The Companion* and *The Listener*.**
4. **The Savior:** *The Savior* is on a mission to save the world and his or her clients! While *The Savior's* assistance can help clients through a rough spot, a dominant *Savior* can lead the coach to become an enabler rather than a companion. **To be in balance, *The Savior* needs to cultivate *The Guide*.**
5. **The Dreamer:** *The Dreamer* is a visionary whose gift is helping clients dream a new reality into being. A dominant

Dreamer may be over-zealous in encouraging clients to pursue new opportunities. A high score is desirable for this archetype. **To be in balance, *The Dreamer* needs to cultivate *The Listener*.**

6. **The Listener:** *The Listener* is attentive to the whole person and to the inspiration of the Spirit. It is the essential archetype for spiritual coaches. A high score is desirable for this archetype. **To be in balance, *The Listener* needs to cultivate *The Guide*.**

7. **The Mystic:** *The Mystic* is the contemplative whose ever-deepening relationship with God provides the basis for his or her calling to the ministry of spiritual coaching. Because *Mystics* understand the spiritual realm, they can guide others into this territory; however, they may also be too ethereal sometimes and may need to come down to earth! **To be in balance, *The Mystic* needs to cultivate *The Companion*.**

8. **The Judge:** *The Judge* is perhaps the least helpful archetype in coaching; however, his or her gift is the ability to perceive right and wrong and, at times, steer clients in the most life-giving directions. **To be in balance, *The Judge* needs to cultivate *The Shaman* and *The Companion*.**

9. **The Shaman:** *The Shaman* works with deep intuition and knows how to heal the soul and guide clients through the individuation process into spiritual and psychological wholeness. This is a highly desirable archetype, but *The Shaman* must resist the temptation to share too much of what he or she sees with the client. **To be in balance, *The Shaman* needs to cultivate *The Listener*.**

10. **The Prophet:** *The Prophet* is caught between heaven and earth, between God's perspective and humans' perspective. This archetype is especially helpful to clients dealing with discrimination and other forms of social

injustice; however, *The Prophet's* indignation may prompt him or her to engage in discussion rather than listening. **To be in balance, *The Prophet* needs to cultivate *The Listener*.**

11. **The Guide**: *The Guide* is another essential archetype for coaches. This archetype offers motivation, discernment, and empowerment, but the coach must avoid the temptation of becoming too directive. **To be in balance, *The Guide* needs to cultivate *The Listener* and *The Companion*.**

12. **The Companion**: *The Companion* offers security and emotional safety to clients and often develops strong ties to those he or she serves; however, because of "murky boundaries," the coaching session may become a "chat" rather than a time for soul-work. **To be in balance, *The Companion* needs to cultivate *The Guide*.**

Now return to your original scores to see how they match or vary from the high/low scores given above. *Which archetypes are too strong? Which archetypes are too weak? Which archetypes do you need to cultivate? What archetypes already compensate for high or low scores?*

SUMMARY

- Archetypes are universal patterns that influence our thoughts and behaviors.
- They occur in the world's myths, literature, and history.
- When archetypes are in balance, they help us become our best selves and serve as guides.
- When one archetype is overly dominant, it can be tyrannical, even destructive, to us and others.
- Archetypes often show up in coaching and other forms of inner guidance.

- They reveal much about clients' values, hopes, fears, and challenges.
- To work with clients at an archetypal level, coaches need to understand their own active archetypes.

"Athleta Christi Nobilis"

Saint George's sword
Plunges down the fiery gullet;
His armored heels
Trample coils of scales
And the beast—
Limp-winged,
Blank-eyed—
Is impotent.

***

I, too, would be a dragon-slayer,
A hunter of brutes
And loathsome fiends,
A killer of pitiless ogres.
I would ferret them out
From the dark places,
Wrenching them into the light.
There, exposed for what they are,
They would cringe,
Sniveling and wilting
Under my fierce gaze,
And I would wield my blade
With power,
Withering them
With a victory song,

***

Woman Dreamer, 1989

CHAPTER FOURTEEN

Coaching Archetypes

As in the case of *The Shadow*, archetypes show up when they will, sometimes in a single coaching session and, at others, as a pattern that reveals itself over time. When we note that an archetype seems active, we must resist the temptation to say, "Oh, I see that you were *The Rescuer* in that situation," or, "How might you become *The Sage* when interacting with your team?" Unless your client is well-versed in the world of archetypes, you would be met with a blank stare or an unceremonious, "Huh?" The better approach is to avoid labels and categories and allow your understanding of archetypes to generate powerful questions instead.

Let's start with a simple example. A team leader has signed up for coaching to improve her rapport with her direct reports. When she started at the company — a large department store — a few months earlier, she received a warm welcome. The ten department heads who reported to her were cooperative and came to weekly meetings ready to share sales trends, problems, and innovations. Conversations were lively and open and the meetings began and ended on time, with all agenda items covered. In recent weeks, all this has changed. Staff drift in late, leave early, and are disengaged throughout each meeting. They arrive unprepared and have little to contribute. The mood is one of sullen resentment. You, as coach, are curious.

Several clarifying questions later, it turns out your client had been eager to establish her own brand at the store. Instead of keeping to the meeting format that had worked so well, she decided to take a more informal approach. Under her watch, the meetings now begin with social time, with Catering providing either cake and coffee or wine and cheese, depending on the time of day. After that, time is set aside for personal sharing and icebreakers to build "team spirit." Instead of taking two hours to cover items for discussion, the time allocated is now only one hour. This means that each department head has only six minutes to provide updates. There is no time for any responses.

The problem, of course, is clear. On an archetypal level, your client has been driven by a combination of *The Caregiver* and *The Companion*. You surmise that what the team expects, however, is a *Leader* who can demonstrate attention to detail, direction, efficiency, time management, and decisiveness — in other words, function as *Guide, Listener, Sage,* and *Judge*, in addition to manifesting *The Companion* archetype. While her direct reports appreciate your client's collegial style, you sense that they resent "wasting time" on socializing, especially as they already have an excellent work rapport. As a result of the new meeting format, there is less time for planning, troubleshooting, and keeping each other informed.

Now that you understand the lack of balance in your client's leadership style, you can ask questions that may facilitate a shift in her awareness:

- What connection do you see between the meeting format change and the team's lack of engagement?
- What did you hope to accomplish by introducing refreshments, personal sharing, and icebreakers?
- What do you need from the team?
- What does the team need from you?
- What positive outcomes have emerged from the change in the meeting format?
- What negative outcomes have emerged from the change in the meeting format?
- What leadership qualities might work best with this team?
- Which of these qualities do you already have?

- What leadership qualities still need developing?
- As a result of this conversation, what changes would you like to make to our coaching agreement?

As you can see, there is no mention of archetypes, but these questions reflect the qualities this client needs to cultivate so as to regain her team's respect. If she insists on "mothering" the team rather than leading it, then the client will have to face an even more serious fallout. The disengaged team will soon degenerate into a demoralized team, eventually moving into mutiny and non-performance. However, if she adapts her style to fit the culture, the team will likely start to function again.

When we understand the patterns underlying common archetypes and how archetypes can complement each other, even compensating, at times, for negative qualities, then we can see more clearly how to proceed. Listening to a coaching narrative, we understand the patterns underlying our clients' attitudes and behaviors, together with those of the individuals and groups with whom they interact. When a father complains about his teenage children's poor school performance and lack of motivation, we may see that instead of showing up as *The Parent*, this dad was too ready to be *The Buddy* and never insisted on accountability or consequences. Or when an elderly client complains that her children never visit her, we may recognize *The Orphan*, that pre-heroic archetype so characteristic of those who have never learned to "parent" themselves and who have never embarked on the journey of life. Similarly, when a client is constantly changing jobs and/or partners and is unable to settle down, we know we have met *The Wanderer*.

But simply recognizing archetypal patterns is not enough. When we understand the kaleidoscope of possible archetypes, we can intuit which ones a client might need to accentuate, cultivate, or diminish. Being "in balance" involves having a variety of active archetypes, especially if one archetype is very dominant. Take, for example, a client who happens to be a *Perfectionist*. Over the course of several sessions, you learn that he is a high achiever who values having everything in order, from physical space to computer files. He has a reputation for being both reliable and conscientious and has proven, repeatedly, that he can deliver results. Despite all this, he is experiencing difficulties at home and work. His colleagues fail to meet his expectations, his wife spends more time at the health club than at home, while his children, still in primary school, bring home "Cs."

After recognizing this client's dominant archetype, you ask clarifying questions to see how it manifests in the various areas of his life. As you suspected, your client is being driven by *The Shadow* side of *The Perfectionist* — *The Tyrant!* Although he complains of exhaustion and insomnia, he cannot delegate because he believes that none of his colleagues perform as well as he can. Though co-workers have stepped forward to help with his workload, he consistently finds fault with their efforts and prefers to work independently. At home, things are no different. His wife works part-time as a nurse but has arranged her schedule to be home when the children are home; however, while he expects her to be responsible for the housework, he often finds dishes in the sink, the beds unmade, and piles of laundry awaiting sorting. As for the children, he is afraid they will never amount to anything as they prefer watching video games to studying. Nobody, it seems, measures up.

This *Perfectionist/Tyrant* needs to recognize the impact his expectations are having on everyone around him. By constantly finding fault, he undermines work morale and alienates his family. Without an *Epiphany*, he will continue with the same unconstructive behaviors — judging, criticizing, blaming, complaining.... As you assess the situation, you consider which archetypes would lessen the negative influence of *The Perfectionist*. First on the list is *The Caregiver*. This archetype evokes compassion, empathy, and understanding; it helps us become less judgmental and more willing to consider extenuating circumstances. When *The Caregiver* is activated, our primary concern is the well-being of those around us. Balanced by *The Caregiver*, *The Perfectionist* would be less demanding and more supportive, nurturing, and sympathetic — and better able to deal with interruptions, missed deadlines, and chaos in general. Anyone who has ever cared for others knows that life can be messy, literally and figuratively, and that people must always come before schedules.

Another important archetype for *The Perfectionist* is *The Fool*. *Perfectionists* tend to take themselves seriously and have little fun in their lives; constantly concerned with appearances, they have forgotten what it is to play. This is where *The Fool* comes in — not *The Shadowy Fool* with its debauchery and obscenities, but *The Wise Fool* who knows how to romp and caper around, how to relax, laugh and enjoy life. Here, in the West, many of us suffer from an insufficiency of Fool; frenetic and uptight, we take ourselves way too seriously. Shackled to our calendars, we have lost all sense of spontaneity, doing nothing unless it is scheduled. Interestingly enough, *The Wise Fool* and *The Tyrant* cannot co-exist simply because *The Wise Fool* — like *The Court Jester* — knows how to speak Truth to Power and how to puncture inflated egos.

Then comes *The Child*. Not the spoiled, whiny brat that represents *The Shadow* side of *The Child*, but *The Holy Child,* who, filled with wisdom and grace, is still connected to the world of Spirit. This archetype will help *The Perfectionist* connect to the world of imagination, fantasy, and play, where all of us can be our authentic selves, accepting others with curiosity rather than judgment.

As coach, you will be aware of your client's driving archetypes and will also see which additional archetypes may help him become more balanced. Unless the client becomes self-aware, however, none of this will matter very much. Instead of explaining *your* insights, you need to help the client experience his own epiphanies — and there may be many! After all, *The Perfectionist* is affecting everyone around him, and that means your questions must be all-encompassing. I have divided the sample questions into two groupings to represent the worlds of work and home.

WORK

- Why is "being perfect" so important to you?
- How do you typically react when your co-workers make mistakes or settle for mediocre results?
- In what ways do you show your displeasure?
- How do your co-workers react when you criticize their work or show your frustration?
- What do you hope to accomplish by making critical comments?
- What is the outcome when you criticize or chastise your colleagues?
- What extenuating circumstances might explain your co-workers' lack of perfection?
- How might you build up morale in the workplace?
- How can you develop meaningful relationships with your co-workers?
- What would help you and your co-workers build more trust and collegiality?
- In what ways might you need to change to experience less frustration?
- In what ways might your colleagues need to change if they wish to produce quality work?
- Who is responsible for "quality control" in the workplace?
- How might your work team take collective ownership of quality control?

- What would it be like to share the burden of quality control with your co-workers?
- What would it be like to accept help from your co-workers when you feel overwhelmed?
- In what ways might your supervisor take more responsibility for ensuring quality control?
- How might you approach your supervisor without sounding as though you want his or her job?
- What "fun" activities or relaxed department policies might foster a happier work environment?

HOME

- Why is it so important for you to have a "perfect" home?
- What needs to change for your home to be "perfect"?
- Who has the time to make these changes?
- What can you contribute towards keeping your home the way you want it to be?
- How might you and your wife decide upon a more equitable division of labor?
- How might your children help more?
- What are the "triggers" that upset you?
- What might be more important than perfection?
- How does your wife react when you are critical of her housekeeping?
- How does your wife react when you are critical of her?
- How do your children react when you criticize them?
- In what ways might you be more encouraging and supportive towards your wife and children?
- How could you have more fun as a family?
- What games might you play with your children?
- How might you help them with their homework?
- How could you help homework become more fun?

- Is there at least one night a week when you and your wife could have a "date night"?
- In what ways do you need to change to create a happier home?
- How can you show your children that you love them unconditionally despite "C" grades?
- How can you show your wife that you love her unconditionally despite the messy house?

Questions like these encourage the client to consider the negative impact he is having on his co-workers, wife, and children. Spread over multiple coaching sessions, these questions allow the client to consider whether he is willing to change and what the results might be should he do so. Again, the coach avoids using archetypal labels, but instead relies on an archetypal framework for approaching the client's many issues. If you want to test this, go back to the two lists of questions and guess which archetype the coach calls upon with each question. For example, "Why is 'being perfect' so important to you?" invites *The Perfectionist* to speak, while "How could you help homework become more fun?" invites the client to consider embracing *The Fool* as an antidote to being uptight and rigid.

A similar approach is possible whenever you observe that a client is driven by *The Shadow* side of an archetype. For example, clients driven by *The Wanderer* are so addicted to exploration and adventure that they may neglect their responsibilities to indulge their wanderlust. Often individualists and rebels, they are not team players but are happiest without rules, regulations, and authority figures. The coaching antidote is to cultivate *The Ruler, The Sage,* and *The Nurturer*. As its name suggests, *The Ruler* relies on reason, laws, and regulations to create and maintain order. *The Sage* instills wisdom and common sense, allowing *The Wanderer* to "wake up" to his or her folly and its accompanying consequences to self and others. *The Nurturer*, on the other hand, awakens sensitivity to the needs of others while reducing inclinations toward selfishness.

Another example is *The Warrior*, that strong, fearless protector who, like *The Hero*, fights evil forces and uses Might for the cause of Right. All this is noble and exemplary, but when *Warriors* become ruthless, controlling, and overbearing, they often rely on excessive force instead of reason/mediation. Here, the coaching antidote is cultivating *The Caregiver*, *The Ruler*, and *The Nurturer*. These three archetypes ensure that *The Warrior* stays within the bounds of how to act with restraint.

And then there is *The Orphan*. While on the positive side, *The Orphan* can offer empathy and understanding, especially in sad or tragic situations, *The Shadow* side of this archetype perpetually wants to be taken care of, expects to be rescued, feels abandoned, and is clueless when it comes to accessing inner power. The coaching antidote is to cultivate *The Warrior*, *The Wanderer*, and *The Wounded Healer*. Instead of playing *The Victim*, now *The Orphan* can fight for his or her rights, go on life's journey, and use the wisdom learned from personal wounds to heal the wounds of others.

SUMMARY

- Archetypes show up when they will, sometimes in a single coaching session and, at others, as a pattern that reveals itself over time.
- The best coaching approach is to avoid archetypal labels and generate powerful questions instead.
- Coaches can generate archetypal questions that facilitate a shift in awareness.

- Listening to a coaching narrative helps us understand the patterns underlying our clients' attitudes and behaviors.
- Being "in balance" involves having a variety of active archetypes, especially if one archetype is excessively dominant.

"Microcosm"

I hold
And am held by
Pieces of life
Ancient as humanity,
Fragments of memory
Which unfold wonders
Teaching totemic ways,
Revealing my place
In the heart of things.
I have learned
Syllables of power
Wielded by shamans
During hidden rites,
Words sacred as spilled blood,
Precious as seeds
In furrowed fields.
I know how to placate
The gods,
When to turn their wrath
And deflect their gaze
Before fury erupts
In floods and fire.

***

I hold
And am held by
Mystery
Older than the race
Yet always new,
Always deepening,

Drawing me
Into that sanctuary
Wider than the skies
More expansive
Than consciousness
Yet somehow contained
Within the reality
I call myself.

***

I hold all
And am held by all
In the cosmic embrace
Which only lovers know.

Woman Dreamer, 1989

CHAPTER FIFTEEN

The Archetype of *The Self*

The False Self versus the Real Self

Throughout this discussion of *Epiphany Moments*, I have distinguished between the *Real Self* and the *False Self*, drawing on sources as diverse as Plato and Farid Ud-Din Attar. Most will agree that humans are born "real," but as Wordsworth points out in *Ode on Intimations of Immortality*, we soon become disconnected from the "clouds of glory" that accompanied us into this world. Instead of remembering the heavenly home from whence we came, "shades of the prison-house" begin to grow around us, especially as we learn to copy the adult world, playing various parts as if our "whole vocation/Were endless imitation." Wordsworth laments that our "visionary gleam" is now dulled by our attachment to "business, love or strife"; these distractions bring forgetfulness, the inability to remember our divine origins or to understand the immensity of our souls. Instead, we settle for the "inevitable yoke," that burden "heavy as frost."

And what kind of self remains when the growing child —Nature's priest — can no longer see the Light because it has faded "into the light of common day"? This self, as we have seen, is prone to *Shadow* possession, whether we call this blocks, the *False Self*, addictions, unbalanced archetypes, or avoidance of Truth. It is a self that suffers because of its dependence upon material goals and possessions and because of its insatiable desire to have more of everything. Fear drives this self, especially the fear of loss, for it feeds on what it owns and on accolades for its supposed accomplishments. Nor can it tolerate diminishment of any kind or being eclipsed by anyone else. It is a competitive self, a jealous self, a greedy self, a punitive self, an unforgiving self, a narcissistic self — and when given free rein, it tramples on others, especially those who shine more brightly or stand in its way. This underdeveloped self is pitiable, for it mistakes illusion for reality and self-deification for religion.

Conversely, the *Real Self* is the *Self* that learns to SEE. Even if this *Self* dwells for a while in a place of "unseeing," its desire for Truth and its hunger for authenticity ensure that it will eventually discover all it seeks. Sometimes, to be sure, moments of "unseeing" dominate but eventually, sight returns, reminding the *Real Self* of its higher calling. This *Self* dares embark on the Quest, despite trepidation; it is willing to endure losses, persecution, and being stripped of any vestiges of comfort. This is a humble *Self*, a grateful *Self*, a vulnerable *Self*, a resilient *Self*, a forgiving *Self*; it is a *Self* driven by curiosity and by the desire for happy endings. Filled with wonder at the beauty of creation, this *Self* knows it is connected to all living beings and that the survival of one species is necessary for the survival of all. This *Self* is also committed to serving others. Precisely because it is aware of the amazing grace that has saved it from its own errors of judgment, this *Self* feels called to share what it has learned for the well-being of all. While the *False Self* is still enmired in its wants, the *Real Self* is self-actualized or, as Jung might say, "individuated."

The Self with a Capital S

In *Man and His Symbols*, Mary Louise Von Franz explains that at the heart of this individuation process lies the "conscious coming to terms with one's own inner center (psychic nucleus) or *Self*," which generally begins with "a wounding of the personality and the suffering that accompanies it" (Jung, p.169). Jung's "*Self*" with a capital "S" seems to be synonymous with the self that must be purified if it is to encounter the Holy One.

We saw in Chapter 10 that Attar's thirty birds must acquiesce to a terrible journey of purgation if they are to reach the court of their spiritual king, the Simorgh. Each bird must be stripped of its primary addiction before it can discover that the One they seek has always resided within each of them. It is only the new, purified *Self* that can understand this. As in other mystical texts, union with the Divine is only possible when we are finally free of the limiting ego and when our baser selves are purified through radical detachment. The Spiritual Quest thus becomes a quest for the elusive *Self* — a terrifying journey of ego abandonment that eventually leads to bliss.

As a spiritual concept, Jung's *Self* could be viewed as the archetype of *The Perfect Human*. In theistic traditions, the *Self* is where we encounter the Divine spark within, where *Atman* (individual soul) and *Brahman* (world soul) are one. For Christians, the *Self* is represented by the person of Christ, who is himself a paradigm of individuation; in contrast, for Buddhists, the *Self* would be "Buddha consciousness," or freedom from desire. *And for our clients?*

The truth of the matter is that unless our clients have signed up for Spiritual Coaching, concepts such as *The Spiritual Quest*, individuation, and encountering the *Self* are unlikely to be agenda items for even a single session, let alone for an extended contract. Typically, clients seek coaching for more "practical" reasons — developing team management skills, improving communication, preparing for retirement, exploring a career change, assessing the viability of a new business, or weighing a decision.

As coaches, our task is to collaborate with our clients so they reach their desired goals, designing the steps and accountability measures that will ensure their success. *But is this all?* Technically speaking, AI can accomplish many of the same outcomes. To test this, I posted the following request on ChatGPT:

ChatGPT

> **CLIENT:** "Please help me decide if I should accept a job offer from a competing firm. I'm a graphic designer for a large publishing house, and I signed a non-compete agreement when I was hired. My company is facing financial difficulties and laying off employees, and my job is insecure. At the same time, I love my colleagues and the projects I am responsible for. In my new position, I would have to do more data entry and less design, which does not thrill me."
>
> **AI COACH:** "It sounds like you're facing a tough decision with both pros and cons on either side. Let's break it down."

Here are the pros of staying with your current company:

1. You love your colleagues and your projects.
2. You're familiar with the company culture and processes.
3. You have job security for now, although the company is facing financial difficulties.

Here are the cons of staying with your current company:

1. Your job is insecure due to layoffs and financial issues.
2. There may be limited growth opportunities if the company continues to struggle.
3. You might face increased workloads or shifts in responsibilities due to layoffs.

Here are the pros of accepting a job offer from the competing firm:

1. Job security — you're moving to a more stable position.

2. You'll have the opportunity to explore new opportunities and expand your skill set.
3. Even though the position involves more data entry, it could lead to opportunities for growth and advancement.

Here are the cons of accepting a job offer from the competing firm:

1. You'll be leaving behind colleagues and projects you enjoy.
2. The new role involves less design work, which may not align with your passions and skills.
3. There could be legal ramifications due to the non-compete agreement you signed, so review that carefully.

Chat GPT's Conclusions

Considering these factors, it seems like you're torn between the stability and security of the new job versus your attachment to your current position. It's essential to weigh these factors carefully and consider your long-term career goals. If you pursue the new opportunity, handle the transition professionally and seek legal advice.

OpenAI. (2024). *ChatGPT* (3.5) [Large language model]. https://chat.openai.com.

This is impressive! The AI coach expresses sympathy in the very first line and then mirrors back what it has heard with 100% accuracy. Not only is the AI coach able to break down the client's dilemma into pros and cons, but it also adds some additional insights. For example, it points out that the client may face increased workloads by staying with the present employer and advises the client to seek legal advice. Here, the AI coach functions more as an advisor than a coach and, instead of eliciting ideas from the client, is overly directive.

While those just setting out on the spiritual journey may be thrilled with this input, those responding to life from the vantage point of the *Self* would not. What is missing from this exchange is soul work. If someone needed quick input to help make a decision, then an AI coach could be useful. If, however, the client is looking for a process that explores different dimensions of decision-making and what this new opportunity means on a soul level, then he or she would be disappointed. The possibility of an *Epiphany Moment* is slim because the AI coach is programmed to yield results, not an experience. But let's test this. Using the same prompt, I asked the AI coach to help me understand what the soul needs in this situation. This was the reply:

AI COACH: It sounds like you are facing a significant decision that involves not only your career but also your emotional well-being and fulfillment. When grappling with such choices, connecting with your inner self and understanding what truly resonates with you is essential.

Here are some questions to help you tap into what your soul wants in this situation:

1. **What ignites your passion?** Reflect on what aspects of your work bring you the most joy and fulfillment. Is it the creative process of graphic design, the camaraderie with your colleagues, or the sense of purpose from working on meaningful projects?
2. **What are your core values?** Consider what values are most important to you in your work and life. Is it stability, creativity, growth, or something else? How do these values align with the options before you?
3. **How do you envision your future?** Visualize where you see yourself in the next few years. Which path feels more aligned with your long-term goals and aspirations? Does

staying with your present company offer potential for growth despite its current challenges, or does the new opportunity provide a clearer path forward?
4. **What does your intuition tell you?** Pay attention to your gut feeling or intuition about each option. Sometimes, our inner voice can provide valuable guidance even when the rational mind is uncertain.
5. **Are you willing to step out of your comfort zone?** Consider whether you're open to embracing change and stepping into the unknown. Growth often requires stepping out of our comfort zones, but assessing whether the potential rewards outweigh the discomfort is essential.
6. **How do you prioritize your well-being?** Remember to consider your overall well-being, including your mental, emotional, and physical health. Which option contributes more positively to your overall well-being and sense of fulfillment?

Ultimately, listening to your inner voice and honoring what feels authentic and true to yourself can guide you in making the decision that aligns best with your soul's desires. Trust yourself and know that whatever choice you make will be a step forward on your journey of growth and self-discovery."

OpenAI. (2024). *ChatGPT* (3.5) [Large language model]. https://chat.openai.com.

Again, I am amazed at the AI coach's wisdom. It summarizes what it has heard, even capturing spiritual nuances. Imagining myself as the client, I experience the AI coach's empathy and feel understood. The questions are powerful "coaching questions" and lead me into deep reflection: *What aspect of my work brings me the most joy? What path feels most aligned with my long-term goals and aspirations? Am I willing to step out of my comfort zone?* While there is no mention of "God" or "Higher Power," and while the material is delivered as a monologue, even so, the *Self* — my *Self* — is hungry for more.

Rocky.AI

AI coach has provided helpful suggestions and plenty to mull over, but, still, is this enough? If the *Self* longs for coaching encounters that go beyond the surface, bringing about new mindfulness and new awakenings, can a Coach Bot really replace a human coach? I gave AI coaching one more try, downloading Rocky.AI from Google Play. This Coach Bot wanted to know my name and initiated our session by narrowing down what I was looking for. When I indicated that I was interested in exploring vision and purpose, my friend Rocky generated options for my selection, responding to each in a "real-time" dialogue. Fascinated, I listened to his comments as he informed me — in a male British accent, no less — that "The essence of coaching is being asked the right questions." Hmm. I mostly agreed with that and was surprised that I was already responding to him as if he were a "he" and not an "it."

Without missing a beat, Rocky told me how amazed he was that I understood my personal values. More praise followed. Then, before I had time to bask in the kudos, he informed me that we needed to get "super strategic" and discuss what it meant to live purposefully. "It's time to get down to actions for the ultimate empowerment," he said. I missed answering several rapidly fired questions, so Rocky defined what having a sense of purpose meant. "You feel a sense of purpose when you use your strengths, talents, and passions to help others," he explained. Apparently, the only limits to my potential were the ones I imposed on myself. In response to my slow reactions, Rocky outlined the next steps to gain clarity, courage, and confidence. He advised me to reflect on my strengths, talents, and passions and to surround myself with like-minded individuals. Oh, and if all that was not enough,

I was to check out his tips and helpful articles and take a self-assessment test.

So how does the *Self* feel about this coaching experience? Testimonials on Rocky.AI's website express how uncannily human Rocky's responses are, how helpful he is when it comes to reaching one's life's vision and goals, and how comforting his support and encouragement can be when one is depressed. But the *Self* is not fooled. The *Self* knows that Rocky is a bot, not a human and that any emotional support he offers is programmed to target generic situations. Unlike a human coach who is (ideally) present in the moment with each client, listening with heart and mind to the coaching narrative, Rocky can only respond to a limited number of questions and answers from a limited repertoire of comments and suggestions. Now, this, in itself, is truly amazing, but for all his talents, Rocky cannot facilitate an *Epiphany Moment* because of the missing ingredient I mentioned earlier — the soul.

Something magical can happen when a human coach meets with a human client. I say "can" because not every coaching session meets its full potential, especially if either the coach or the client fails to be engaged. But let's return to the magic, to a "best case" scenario. When two humans risk being vulnerable in a space of trust, safety, and mutual positive regard, they share the same energy field. There is no "I"/"Thou" but only a "We"; a shared experience of the present moment in which yesterday and tomorrow become irrelevant and all walls tumble down. In this moment, there is no separation but a kind of communion, for want of a better term, a union of hearts and minds, an at-one-ness of Spirit. Both participants in this union know they have been grasped by "something" larger than themselves, even if they never articulate this. Words, in fact, would destroy the experience, as would any attempt to define it. They can *feel* it but not see it; they know it is happening but don't feel the need to draw attention to it.

But if one is uncomfortable with spiritual language, brain science offers alternative wording. In my book, *Mind-Shifting Imagery: Image Guidance for Life Coaches*, I point out that "Neuroscience research suggests that the deepest levels of communication happen when brains 'couple' or connect through listening/speaking activities" (Stewart, p.27). Citing the research of Princeton University neuroscientists Uri Hasson, Lauren J. Silbert, and Greg J. Stephens, I explain that such "neural coupling" allows the listener — in this case, the coach — to be so connected to the speaker — in this case, the client — that he or she can anticipate what the speaker is going to say next. In such situations, the client feels heard precisely because the coach's brain activity mirrors the speaker's. I conclude, "In fact, the greater the anticipatory coupling, the greater the understanding between speaker and listener" (Stewart, p.27).

The coach listens and receives, "crossing-over" into the client's lived experience, providing fertile space for exploration and discovery, asking questions and considering answers. *Chronos* stands still, and instead of being driven by the clock, the coaching session unfolds in *Kairos*, that timeless dimension of time in which the soul is most at home. There is no rush, no pushing to ask the "right" questions, no attempt at directing, influencing, or sounding clever. Rather, as stories unfold, the coach keeps vigil, tending the sacred fire of Truth, responding briefly, simply, and authentically. Every now and again, the coach mirrors back the essence of what the client is sharing or asks a clarifying question; occasionally, the coach may share an observation or ask permission to offer a suggestion. This is the client's time; the goal is not so much to drive an agenda as to open up new vistas of possibility, along with more expansive opportunities for growth — and for *Epiphany Moments*! For the client, experiencing the undivided care and attention of another human being is a gift indeed! In the stillness, the client finds the space to reflect, imagine, and reach understanding.

The dialogue that ensues is not so much a dialogue between coach and client as between the client and the client's *Self* (or emerging *Self*). The coach's role is to witness and sometimes facilitate the client's process of inner discovery. As the client re-frames experiences and de-constructs erroneous assumptions, the coach is there to validate and be supportive; as the client wrestles with difficult decisions or re-visits painful situations, the coach offers encouragement while expressing empathy, even praise. If the client is overwhelmed, the coach can ask questions that, evoking awareness or insight, help the client move beyond current thinking.

And if the future seems like unchartered territory, the coach and client together can generate ideas about "next steps" that are appropriate, achievable, and meaningful. At the end of the session or of the contracted sessions, the client is conscious of having changed. Not only has coaching delivered the desired agenda outcomes, but the client now perceives the world through new lenses. The contemplative pacing, the sense of being "held," the pointed questions, the moments of silence, the neural coupling — all these factors have literally stripped the old self away, allowing the *Self* to emerge for the first time or, if it has been hibernating, to re-appear once again.

Concluding Thoughts

Coaching is both a journey and a destination that involves a creative partnership between the coach, client, and all stakeholders. The process of exploring stated goals and desires in a safe, supportive environment unlocks new insights and opportunities for growth, allowing the client to reach for the most desirable possible outcomes. At its best, coaching leads to a mind shift, a change in perspective. It is not about maintaining the *status quo* but about diving deeper, gaining clarity, understanding oneself, becoming more authentic, and encountering Truth. This leads me to wonder, can coaching be coaching if there is no *Epiphany Moment*, or, at least, if the individual session or the contracted time lacks movement toward revelation, discovery, awareness, intuition, perception, and insight? Can coaching be coaching if coach and client part company without having experienced a shared "Ah-ha" moment or, as Archimedes would say, a powerful "Eureka"?

If coaching is merely a matter of following the "agenda formula," then perhaps it is time to call in the Coaching Bots!

FINAL QUESTIONS FOR CONSIDERATION

Q1: When Epiphany Moments come your way, you tend to:

1. Welcome them enthusiastically.
2. Acknowledge them reluctantly.
3. Deny they are happening.
4. Reach for the Pepto-Bismol.
5. Run in the opposite direction.

Q2: When your clients are about to have an Epiphany, you tend to:

1. Stay silent.
2. Ask powerful questions.
3. Dissect what is happening.
4. Maintain a neutral presence.
5. Try to speed up the process.

Q3: When your clients share an experience of Epiphany, you tend to:

1. Listen attentively and validate the experience.
2. Analyze what actually happened.
3. Focus on the contracted goals.

4. Suggest that therapy might be in order.
5. Remind your clients that you are a coach, not a guru.

Q4. The main reason people fear Epiphany Moments is because:

1. They reveal unpleasant truths about ourselves.
2. They invite us to change.
3. They puncture our egos.
4. They call us to break free of the status quo.
5. They demand authenticity and strip us of our public personas.

"INSIGHT"

The truth about me
Is that I'm a poet—
A crafter of words
Lured by magic
And Mystery,
By paradox
And uncertainty.
My slice of life
Is intensely buttered
On both sides,
Layered with *epiphanies*
Great and small,
Spread with ambiguity,
Riddled with enigmas
And breaks in consciousness.

***

When words come,
I am possessed by words:
They spew forth
As burning prophecy,
Relentless in urgency,
Generous in clarity.
They sear my lips
Like Isaiah's coal,
Choke me like the scroll
On which Ezekiel fed,
Until, emptied and poured out,
I find silence.

***

It is not so much the words
That matter
As their hidden source
Deep within
The core of self,
Deeper than abstract conventions
Or poetic license,
Deeper, too, than dexterity.
More seductive
Than art or logic,
Power or prestige.

***

I speak of the smithy
Of a poet's soul,
That place where words
Are forged from grace,
Hammered by truth,
Nailed by pain,
That place where the interplay
Of light and darkness
Creates both gift and curse,
Laughter and anguish.

***

The truth about me
Is that I know
How to weep
And how to dream
How to wonder

And be surprised
Into joy.

***

I am both poem and poet,
One who holds
The editorial pen
To censor the self
So words may be
And so, through them,
The Spirit may dance
Into the hearts of humankind.

***

Woman Dreamer, 1989

References

Anthony, Scott D. "Kodak's Downfall Wasn't About Technology." *Harvard Review,* July 15, 2016. https://hbr.org/2016/07/kodaks-downfall-wasnt-about-technology.

Aristotle, Horace, Longinus. *Classical Literary Criticism.* Middlesex, UK: Penguin Classics, 1965.

Association for Psychological Science. "Can Fetus Sense Mother's Psychological State? Study Suggests Yes." *ScienceDaily.* 10 November 2011.

Attar, Farid Ud-Din. *The Conference of the Birds.* Middlesex, UK: Penguin Classics, 1984.

Auden, W. H. "The Unknown Citizen." Perrine, Laurence (ed.). *Literature: Structure, Sound and Sense.* New York: Harcourt Brace Jovanovich, Inc., 1984.

Campbell, Joseph (ed.). *The Portable Jung.* New York: Viking Penguin, Inc., 1971.

Clutterbuck, David. *Coaching the Team at Work.* London: Nicholas Brealey Publishing, 2020.

Hahn, Thich Nhat. *The Miracle of Mindfulness.* Massachusetts: Beacon Hill Press, 1975.

Harrison, G. B. (ed.). *Shakespeare: The Complete Works.* New York: Harcourt, Brace & World, Inc., 1968.

Ibsen, Henrik. "A Doll's House." Henderson, Gloria, William Day and Sandra Waller (eds.). *Literature and Ourselves.* New York: Harper Collins, 1994.

Johnson, Robert A. *Owning Your Own Shadow*: *Understanding the Dark Side of the Psyche.* New York: HarperCollins, 1991.

Jung, Carl G. *Man and his Symbols.* New York: Dell Publishing, Co. Inc., 1984.

Lawrence, D. H. "The Rocking Horse Winner." Pickering, James H. and Jeffrey D. Hoeper (eds.). *Literature.* New York: Macmillan Publishing Company, 1994.

References

O'Connor, Flannery. "Revelation." Henderson, Gloria, William Day and Sandra Waller (eds.). *Literature and Ourselves*. New York: Harper Collins, 1994.

Plato. "Allegory of the Cave." Henderson, Gloria, William Day and Sandra Waller (eds.). *Literature and Ourselves*. New York: Harper Collins, 1994.

Sophocles. "Oedipus Rex." Henderson, Gloria, William Day and Sandra Waller (eds.). *Literature and Ourselves*. New York: Harper Collins, 1994.

Stewart, Elizabeth-Anne. *Mind-Shifting Imagery: Image Guidance for Life Coaches*. Chicago: 2018.

Stewart, Elizabeth-Anne. *Jesus the Holy Fool*. Wisconsin: Sheed & Ward, 1999.

Thomas, Dylan. "Fern Hill." Pickering, James H. and Jeffrey D. Hoeper (eds.). *Literature*. New York: Macmillan Publishing Company, 1994.

Vanek (Stewart), Elizabeth-Anne. *Woman Dreamer*. Indiana: Wyndham Hall Press, 1989.

Vanek (Stewart), Elizabeth-Anne. *Extraordinary Time*. Ohio: Life Enrichment Publishers, 1988.

Vanek (Stewart), Elizabeth-Anne. *Frost and Fire*. Ohio: Life Enrichment Publishers, 1985.

Wordsworth, William. "Ode on Intimations of" in Palgrave, F.T. (ed.). *The Golden Treasury*. London: Oxford University Press, 1963.

About the Author

Dr Elizabeth-Anne Stewart
Professional Certified Coach; Board Certified Coach

More than ever, the world needs spiritual guidance. *"Things fall apart; the center cannot hold,"* wrote W. B. Yeats in the aftermath of World War I. No matter how dire the predictions, I believe we can move beyond fear and apathy into a future of possibilities.

***

Born in England and raised both in England and on the tiny Mediterranean island of Malta, I have always been a leader

About the Author

with multiple interests, inexhaustible energy, and a delight in creativity. I love people and especially enjoy the roles of teacher and guide. Nothing pleases me more than to be the midwife of an "Ah-Ha" moment; a catalyst for meaningful change and for growth in awareness.

***

A Professional Certified Coach (PCC-ICF), Board-Certified Coach (BCC), Coach Educator, and Spiritual Director, I have 40+ years of experience offering inner guidance, retreats, and seminars. I hold a PhD in Theology from the University of Malta, Europe, and was trained as a Spiritual Director at the Claret Center, Chicago. I have published 12 books, including *Mind-Shifting Imagery: Image Guidance for Life Coaches*. I also publish *Sunday BibleTalk*, a weekly e-commentary on the Sunday liturgical readings.

***

On faculty at The Institute for Life Coach Training (ILCT — https://www.lifecoachtraining.com), where I also serve as an Assessor and Mentor Coach, I served as Director of Education for *ThrivingTogether*, an ACSTH/Level One grant-funded Ministerial Coach Training Program at The Catholic Theological Union (CTU) from 2021–2023. Following the completion of the grant, I launched The Ministry Coaching Foundation (https://ministrycoachingfoundation.com) to offer continuing education and personal enrichment courses for coaches and ministers, in addition to coach mentoring for groups and individuals. My course in *Transformational Coaching* — approved for 40 ICF CCEUs — has already graduated several cohorts of amazing students. In addition, I teach *Creative Writing* and *Professional Writing* at Saint Xavier University, Chicago.

***

Though I serve primarily in Christian contexts, I work with clients from every faith tradition (or none) and am available for individual and group retreats, motivational seminars, and creativity workshops. My background uniquely positions me to assist teams in exploring their vision/mission, developing communication skills, and, in the case of ministry teams, extending their pastoral reach.

***

As a teacher and spiritual guide, I am committed to expanding consciousness and compassion through the inward journey. My goal is to assist clients connect more deeply with their Divine Source, thereby helping them access the extraordinary capacities within. To this end, I work with those who believe that it is possible to move beyond "bad news" and limiting circumstances to create a new reality, not only for humankind but for all creation. Nicknamed "The Great Motivator" when I taught at DePaul University, I encourage clients to re-discover the fire within, to re-kindle their enthusiasm, and to re-commit to a life of service.

***

https://www.elizabeth-annestewart.com
https://www.ministrycoachingfoundation.com
http://www.chicagowritingcoach.com

Books by Dr Elizabeth-Anne Stewart

Mind-Shifting Imagery: Image Guidance for Life Coaches

A sequel to *Image Guidance: A Tool for Spiritual Direction* (Paulist Press, 1992) and *Image Guidance and Healing* (Paulist Press, 1994), this book provides safe, brief, and effective guidelines for using imagery in coaching, spiritual direction, pastoral counseling, and other forms of inner guidance. ISBN: 9781721576302.

"If you are a coach, therapist, or some other sort of life guide, read this book and keep it handy for times when you feel stuck with a particular client or situation, or even to instill new creativity and energy into your work as a life coach."

Dr Patrick Williams, MCC, BCC. Author of *Becoming a Professional Life Coach: The Art and Science of a Whole Person Approach.*

Preaching & Teaching Laudato Si'

Preaching and Teaching Laudato Si is a primer for preachers, teachers, and others who wish to preach, teach, or reflect on the spiritual implications of a green agenda. It is also a resource for people of any faith who wish to respond to Pope Francis' plea for ecological conversion. ISBN: 97815153788396.

"Dr Stewart's book provides a wide collection of resources that appeal to varied learning styles. Her poetry and images convey her profound appreciation of all creation. Her positive and negative confessions include more than enough suggestions so that each reader can choose an action with which to express their own convictions about our human responsibility for the cosmos."

Sr Dolores Lytle, CSA

A Pocketful of Sundays

This book is a collection of scripturally-based reflections from *Sunday BibleTalk* grouped thematically under seven headings: *Letting Go, Letting God, Following the Way, Dark Night, Thy Kingdom Come, Priests and Prophets, Awake to Life*. It is a resource to be "dipped into" and read contemplatively rather than read "cover to cover." From 1986–2005, I was the Sunday writer for *Living Faith*, a quarterly with a subscription base of over half a million readers. ISBN: 5-80003-0-792242.

Editor Mark Neilsen had this to say about my scripture reflections:

*"No writer of **Living Faith** has been more prolific, more creative, and more original than you have been over the years. It has been a great run, a fantastic effort..."*

The Day the Fireworks Died
Malta, PEG Publications, 2005

It is the *festa* of *San Gorg*, but dark clouds hang over the village of Ta' Qalbi, and none of the fireworks will ignite. Gorg, a village outcast known to his schoolmates as "Hushu Bushu," learns from San Gorg that the saint is displeased with the people of Ta'Qalbi who, though churchgoing, are heartless and corrupt. With the help of Id Dragun, the dragon, Gorg confronts the people of his village, and there is a change of heart all around — as well as fireworks, processions, and marching bands... ISBN:99909-0-4200.

The Maltese Translation/Adaptation, **Id-Dragun tad-Dragonara,** released in 2017, is available from Preca Publications, Malta:

*"Preca Publications of Blata l-Bajda have just published a new book for children and adolescents entitled **Id-Dragun tad-Dragonara**. This is*

*a translation and adaptation into Maltese of **The Day the Fireworks Died**, originally penned in English by Elizabeth-Anne Stewart. The Maltese version is the work of Carmel G. Cauchi, and the full-color illustrations have been done by Frank Schembri."*
The Malta Independent

Dragut's Galley
Malta, PEG Publications, 2004

Sarah and Andrew, two young American teenagers, are visiting their grandparents in Malta, an island in the heart of the Mediterranean with a history of repeated invasions by Turkish corsairs. Excited by the legends of this historic past, they set out to discover their roots and discover a deeper truth than they ever imagined...

Set in contemporary Malta, the author's homeland and sacred landscape, *Dragut's Galley*, is an adventure with a difference that is sure to grip the reader from the very start. Intended for readers 9–14 years of age, as well as for adults who are children at heart, it delivers a positive message much needed in a world divided by religious differences and intolerance. ISBN: 99909-379-4.

Jesus the Holy Fool
Sheed & Ward, 1999

My best-known book is *Jesus the Holy Fool* (Wisconsin: Sheed & Ward, 1999). This is a reverent study of the Gospel Jesus that draws connections between holiness and folly as they occur in the Bible, presenting Holy Foolishness as a paradigm for the Christian journey and as a new model for what it means to be church. In 1999, this book caused controversy in South Africa, where politicians initially misunderstood the meaning of "Holy Fool" and wanted to ban the 1999 *Parliament of the World's Religions* because of my presentation. ISBN: 1-58051-061-2.

"Brings to light ancient wisdom about the mystery of Christ. Reverent and challenging."
   Donald Senior, C.P., **Catholic Theological Union**

"Combines sound theology with creative imagination. Enlightens and delights."
   Marie-Henry Keane, O.P., **Blackfriars Hall, Oxford University**

"A wise, rich, and theologically informed book; a moving invitation to consider an important new dimension of Christology."
   Wayne G. Rollins, **Hartford Seminary**

From Center to Circumference: God's Place in the Circle of Self
Paulist Press, 1996

This book offers a series of brief reflections on the inner life, drawing on my own experiences as a means of illustration. Not meant as mere autobiography, these reflections point beyond personal narrative to universal wisdom. The book can serve as a journaling tool or as a "manual for spiritual direction." The main theme is that it is not enough to allow God a place in one's life; on the contrary, God must be both at the center and circumference of self. ISBN: 0-8091-3623-6.

"Those who read this book will be provoked to gather, reverence, and share their own stories of grace."
   Rev. Louis J. Cameli, **University of St Mary of the Lake**

"Her wisdom, enhanced by many years as a spiritual director, shines through. The reader will feel the sure and gentle touch of her guiding hand."
   Ewert Cousins, **Fordham University**

Image Guidance & Healing
Paulist Press, 1994

This sequel to *Image Guidance: A Tool for Spiritual Direction* includes healthcare possibilities and various case studies. These demonstrate the use of Image Guidance in post-accident rehabilitation, stress-related illnesses, serious conditions such as diabetes and cancer, addictions, and minor ailments with a psycho-spiritual basis. Image Guidance can help clients understand the roots of their illness, addiction, or disability, live in harmony with themselves and their current state of health, relieve stress, and find inner peace. ISBN: 0-8091-3508-6.

"Vanek's (Stewart's) case material provides an excellent embodiment of the image guidance process and helps the reader to appreciate the very real gift she brings to this endeavor."
   Joan E. Bowers, ***Department of Nursing, DePaul University***

"Elizabeth-Anne Vanek (Stewart) is an intuitive healer with an uncanny ability to help her clients express and transform their physical problems through imagery. Extending Jung's technique of active imagination, a type of inner dialogue with spontaneous images, she illustrates how to evoke this healing fantasy in individuals with physiological conditions."
   August J. Cwik, ***Jung Institute, Evanston***

Image Guidance: A Tool for Spiritual Direction
Paulist Press, 1992

Through a series of case studies, I demonstrate how to dialogue with the active imagination so as to use imagery as an intuitive map that will help guide lives and chart the course of spiritual direction. The book provides a step-by-step account of how to work with spontaneous images, how to extract wisdom from dreams, and how to recognize the symbolic significance of mythical themes. Ideally used within a counseling context,

Image Guidance helps us address our problems with greater perception and sensitivity. We learn how to look at past and present experiences, imagine future experiences, and create options for ourselves that we might otherwise have not seen. ISBN: 978-0809133215.

"For those who are attracted by their imaginations to the way of symbols, Elizabeth-Anne Vanek's (Stewart's) book offers privileged access to those symbols that emerge from the depths of the psyche and, with grace and guidance, can lead the spiritual pilgrim toward the goal of the journey."
    Ewert Cousins, **Fordham University**

Woman Dreamer
Wyndham Hall Publishers, 1999

This collection of poems is grounded in archetypal imagery. While some of the themes are distinctly Christian, and while others are shaped by the Hebrew scriptures, still others draw on the world of myth, providing a new twist to stories of creation, fall, and redemption. Many of the poems are mystical in orientation and focus on the relationship between Lover and Beloved, especially on the desire for union and the intense emotions that such yearning entails. A few are set in the landscape of childhood or else explore the territory of pain. Without exception, the poems present a world that is at once recognizable yet surreal, tangible yet elusive, unique yet universal, immediate yet dream-like.

"The reader who follows Vanek's (Stewart's) guidance through scenes of everyday life, through the drama of Biblical narratives, and through the forest of primordial archetypal symbols, will be delighted aesthetically and enriched spiritually."
    Ewert Cousins, **Fordham University**

Pilgrims at Heart
Creative Communications for the Parish, 1993

This pocketbook contains some of my best scripture reflections from *Living Faith*, a quarterly publication that provides brief meditations on the day's readings. My Sunday reflections for *Living Faith* offered insights that came from lived experience rather than from mere book learning. ISBN: 0-9629585-3-0.

"As a person convinced of the truth of faith, Vanek (Stewart) writes with the urgency of one searching for a way to express that faith genuinely in her everyday life. Her insight into the spiritual journey can enrich all of us, no matter where we find ourselves on the pilgrimage to the heart of God."
 The Editors, *Living Faith Publications*

Leaning Into Light

This collection of poetry brings together the best selections from **Frost and Fire** (Ohio: Life Enrichment Publishers, 1985; ISBN: 0-9378736-16-7) and ***Extraordinary Time*** (Life Enrichment Publishers, 1988; ISBN: 0-938736-24-8). Both books, which represent my earliest published work, are out of print; however, I do have multiple copies of this volume available. The poems trace much of my own spiritual journey.

"The most effective prophets are poets. They lead us to truth and goodness through the beautiful. Elizabeth-Anne Vanek (Stewart) is such a prophet. Her poetry helps us to hear the biblical stories anew, to see their settings, and to enter the very flesh and spirit of those who move about seeking God. She helps us to pray biblical prayers, to hear biblical stories as our own stories, and to delight in biblical wisdom as though it were all our own discovery."
 Eugene LaVerdiere, SSS, ***Emmanuel***

"I am again impressed with the delicate touch of beauty and the intense movement of contemplation in your work. I thank you for sharing this gift with us."
    Carroll Stuhlmueller, C.P., **Catholic Theological Union**

"These poems are like favorite melodies transposed into a minor key, haunting the reader with the intimate revelations of the actors and their sudden recognition of the overwhelming presence of God. This book is a very powerful acclamation that sign seeking is universal, and that waiting for what is possible, sometimes in frustration, is worthwhile."
    Linda McCallum Krause, **Currents in Theology and Mission**

CHANGEMAKERS
BOOKS

Transform your life, transform our world. Changemakers Books publishes books for people who seek to become positive, powerful agents of change. These books inform, inspire, and provide practical wisdom and skills to empower us to write the next chapter of humanity's future.

www.changemakers-books.com

Current Bestsellers from Changemakers Books

Resetting Our Future: Am I Too Old to Save the Planet? A Boomer's Guide to Climate Action
Lawrence MacDonald

Why American boomers are uniquely responsible for the climate crisis — and what to do about it.

Resetting Our Future: Feeding Each Other Shaping Change in Food Systems through Relationship
Michelle Auerbach and Nicole Civita

Our collective survival depends on making food systems more relational; this guidebook for shaping change in food systems offers a way to find both security and pleasure in a more connected, well-nourished life.

Resetting Our Future: Zero Waste Living, The 80/20 Way The Busy Person's Guide to a Lighter Footprint
Stephanie J. Miller

Empowering the busy individual to do the easy things that have a real impact on the climate and waste crises.

The Way of the Rabbit
Mark Hawthorne

An immersion in the world of rabbits: their habitats, evolution and biology; their role in legend, literature, and popular culture; and their significance as household companions.